A Fool's Guide to Actual Happiness

A FOOL'S GUIDE TO ACTUAL HAPPINESS

Mark Van Buren

Wisdom

Wisdom Publications
199 Elm Street
Somerville, MA 02144 USA
wisdompubs.org

Library of Congress Cataloging-in-Publication Data
Names: Van Buren, Mark, author.
Title: A fool's guide to actual happiness / Mark Van Buren.
Description: Somerville, MA: Wisdom Publications, 2018. |
    Includes bibliographical references and index. |
Identifiers: LCCN 2017048415 (print) | LCCN 2018005628 (ebook) |
    ISBN 9781614294641 (ebook) |
    ISBN 9781614294481 (pbk.: alk. paper)
Subjects: LCSH: Buddhism—Psychology. | Happiness—Religious
    aspects—Buddhism.
Classification: LCC BQ4570.P76 (ebook) |
    LCC BQ4570.P76 V36 2018 (print) | DDC 294.3/444—dc23
LC record available at https://lccn.loc.gov/2017048415

ISBN 978-1-61429-448-1   ebook ISBN 978-1-61429-464-1

22 21 20 19 18   5 4 3 2 1

Interior design by Kristin Goble. Set in Tisa OT 10/14.

Wisdom Publications' books are printed on acid-free paper and meet
the guidelines for permanence and durability of the Production
Guidelines for Book Longevity of the Council on Library Resources.

❂ This book was produced with environmental mindfulness.
For more information, please visit wisdompubs.org/
wisdom-environment.

Printed in the United States of America.

*This book is dedicated to my wife, Michelle,
and my beautiful children,
Mason Alexander and Madelyn Rose.*

CONTENTS

Section III: Putting It All Together

PREFACE

All beings want to be happy, yet so very few know how.

—SHARON SALZBERG

ALL OF US want actual happiness. But what does this really mean? Where can this "happiness" be found? Allow me to let you in on a little secret. Actual happiness is *now*. It cannot be any other time. If you search for it outside this moment, it will always seem just beyond your reach. In fact, true happiness is your natural state of being, it is your birthright, and it is not gained through forceful effort but is, rather, discovered and realized once you let go of all the things keeping it hidden. As the saying goes, *the sun is always shining behind the clouds.*

Actual happiness is not owned by a certain religion, and everyone has access to it—religious or not—yes, that means you as well! It is so simple and ordinary it's typically overlooked, much like a fish searching for the ocean, or a poor man sitting on a bucket full of money. The truth is we can all learn to rest in this natural state, and it's as simple as paying attention to what's happening in our lives in this very moment—warts and all. Occasionally though, you may catch a glimpse of an inner stillness, like when a beautiful sunset stops you dead in your tracks, or when something so terrifying happens it pulls the rug right out from beneath your feet, leaving you with no choice but to surrender fully to the direct experience of life. In these moments you find a silence within, a peace beyond the conditions you are experiencing—actual happiness! It's as if we become, as poet T.S. Eliot once called it, *the still point of the turning world*. Resting from this still point, you see the world as it rushes by in its ever-changing flux. For me, Buddhism has really helped to see this.

Let me be clear about something from the very beginning: I'm not a meditation master and I'm not a lineage-holding Buddhist teacher. But I am a guy who's really benefited from its teachings. And I'm a guy who just loves to share stuff

I've found useful, and some folks have told me
I have a knack for explaining things in a catchy
way. Oh, and I'm also sometimes kind of a fool.
Let me give you an example.

Early on in my practice I was at a retreat
listening to a Chan master, Guo Ru Fashi, give a
talk about letting go of attachments; a common
theme found throughout all Buddhism. I fool-
ishly thought I knew how I could demonstrate
to him that I was totally free from attachments.
My idea was brilliant. Profound. Really big. I'd
give him a demonstration that would convince
him that I was his star pupil. I was going to fully
extinguish my attachment to myself and to what
people thought of me. So what would I do, you
ask? I would pour a glass of water on my head in
front of the master in my private interview with
him that very afternoon! Because: water *extin-
guishes*. Right?

When it came time for my interview, it
turned out my private interview wasn't so private
after all . . . In the interview room was Guo Ru
Fashi, his translator, a monk, and a very serious-
looking nun. Regardless of the crowd, I still trot-
ted in there with my mug full of water, ignoring
the master's attendant outside the room, who

xii ■ A FOOL'S GUIDE TO ACTUAL HAPPINESS

told me I couldn't bring it with me. There I stood, water in hand, in front of this terrifying troop of serious Buddhist practitioners. Instead of sitting down on my cushion, I kept standing and went on to say, "*All my life I have worried about what other people have thought of me, I am ready to finally let it go.*" With that line, I raised my mug up high and released a mugful of tepid water onto my head. I then proclaimed, "*Now, I'm ready.*" And I prostrated to the master and the watching crowd, flamboyantly staying face down in my prostration.

After a few moments of satisfaction, I decided to come out of my prostration and look up at the master, who I was certain would be impressed and beaming. He was not. Nor was he (or were any of the onlookers) amused. I followed up my performance by asking if I could borrow a towel.

Guo Ru Fashi then generously went on to explain how letting go isn't shown by some external display but is more of an internal letting go into our self-nature; it cannot be proven by putting on some show.

Although this was straight-up foolish—no doubt about it—it was also quite liberating in its own awkward kind of way. I realized I wasn't afraid of looking like a fool. For once, I actually wasn't afraid to just be my foolish self.

Shunryu Suzuki Roshi once called walking the path "one continuous mistake"—and this has definitely been true for me. But it's also had a really profound impact on my life. It has brought to me what I can only call actual happiness.

I have now been practicing the Buddhist path for a good while, around ten years—although it's not long in the cosmic scheme of things, I do take this path seriously (even if I do that with a sense of humor)—and I am confident this book and the practices it points to have something of substance to offer. Although I still consider myself a fool of sorts when it comes to the practice, I also think that sharing some of what I've learned might be helpful to you as a spiritual companion on the path. If you are just starting out, perhaps I may be a few steps ahead of you and can help you avoid some of the traps I fell into when I first began and maybe point out a few of the sights. If you've been at this a while, maybe I can be a fellow traveler walking beside you on the path—possibly offering a fresh, new perspective on old teachings.

So what do you think? Shall we walk together?

INTRODUCTION

We are no longer happy as soon as we wish to be happier.
—WALTER S. LANDOR

ONE DAY I was listening to a talk given by a Buddhist teacher when a woman in the audience shared her experience: no matter how much she meditated and was aware of herself throughout the day, she was still just her same old shitty self. Her brutally honest confession cloaked in humor made me sit up and take notice. Finally, here was someone who felt the same way I did! I didn't know this woman, had never met her, but I was sure as hell relieved to hear someone else was struggling like I was. It seemed that despite her efforts to better herself, she wasn't making the progress she expected. I had been worrying about the same thing. But since then, after much reflection and self-study, I have come to realize that what I need to do is just *be my own shitty self*. More than that, though, I've realized my path is to be completely and fully myself—exactly who I am with all my neuroses and suffering, along with all my capacities for love and joy. No more struggling or running away from who I actually am, no more trying to be someone I'm not.

After many years of education, training, and yes, battling my own high expectations, I arrived at the understanding that I don't have to try so hard to be at peace with myself and my life. This was the catalyst for writing this book: I wanted to share my journey with you—and I hope you too may have the chance to liberate yourself from that which shackles you.

There is no perfect person you have to become—and no one you have to idolize. The only role models you need to look up to are those willing to face themselves and their lives honestly and openly. In time, you may find that by not trying so hard to change for the better, your own self-transformation will naturally occur.

The concepts and practices presented in this book have brought about a more profound sense of peace within me—and I'm betting they might for you too. I believe that you too can learn to strive less and just be—and gradually live your way into a more deeply fulfilled existence, no longer resisting pain and uncertainty but welcoming even those things as opportunities to be free. More importantly, I hope you can stop trying so hard and learn to accept that your shitty, foolish self is—at its deepest level—already good enough, overflowing with enoughness.

SECTION I

Concepts & Beliefs

1
SELF-HELP
OR SELF-HATE?

Better is the enemy of good.
—A RECENT FORTUNE COOKIE

THERE ARE THOUSANDS of self-help books out on the market right now: books to help you become a "better person" in order to finally be happy in your life; books that say if you just keep working on yourself, you'll finally make it, you'll finally get it all together; books that say if you follow these Three Easy Steps, you'll be healthy, wealthy, and problem-free for the rest of your life. This is *not* one of those books. I am not here to give you a permanent solution to all your problems, nor can the words in this book magically make you or your life somehow "better" per se. There's no way that I—or anyone else for that matter—can remove the inevitable pains and difficulties we *all* will have to experience at some point amid our messy lives. Rather, I hope that through sharing concepts, tools, and practices I've implemented in my own life, you will have a realistic roadmap to *actual* happiness. By holding the possibility for you to be completely awake and at ease with all the ten thousand joys and sorrows of your life, I truly believe you, too, have the potential to find a perfect peace right at the center of all your imperfections.

I want to show you how everything you encounter can be used as a path of awakening to the wisdom you *already have* within you—and how whatever arises in your life can be used to cultivate love and compassion for yourself and all beings. More importantly, I'd like you to put down the burden of trying so hard to become an idealized version of yourself—and instead move toward deeply experiencing each and every unique moment of your unique existence. Like all of us, sometimes you will feel incredible and other times you will feel absolutely horrible—yet being fully present through it all with an evenness of mind, and without getting stuck in wishing for things to be different, is the only way to live deeply, the only way to real peace. And really, if you're not present with the direct experience of your life in this moment, regardless of the circumstances, are you really living at all?

Don't get me wrong: working with yourself, in and of itself, is not a problem—and it's definitely part of the practice. The problem is that the idea of becoming *better* usually comes from a subtle form of aggression toward yourself. The same is true of the belief that something is wrong with who you already are: this too is a form of self-directed aggression. Both are self-hatred and aversion cleverly disguised as something seemingly positive—and when we get taken in by that disguise, we diminish the possibility of contentment and self-acceptance. This self-hatred runs deep within our culture and sneaks its way into many wonderful tools and practices originally intended to liberate you, such as mindfulness and meditation. So often, when we begin these inward processes, we pervert them into just another way to manufacture ammunition to use against ourselves. These practices, originally designed to work with thoughts and emotions in a healing way, seem to produce adverse effects. We wind up becoming angry and impatient with ourselves for having so many thoughts, or we find ourselves stuck in a continuous struggle with emotional baggage that won't just magically go away. Happens to me too! I still struggle with this whenever the idea to be "better" than who I already am infiltrates my mind—but over the years I've learned to see a little more deeply into the nature of these ideas. I've noticed the suffering they've caused me whenever I've grabbed hold of them, and have found practical ways to finally let them go.

Becoming a "better" person also has the tendency to develop into perfectionism and leads to the avoidance of negative emotions, thoughts, and situations through a type of "pretending it's all okay." This creates loads of dualities, such as right and wrong, good and bad, "shoulds" and "shouldn'ts," generating strict rules and regulations that leave you constantly feeling guilty about not living up to your "ideal" or "better" self. We've all been sucked into believing this idea that we are not good enough, that we need to be fixed. We're brainwashed into believing this in countless ways.

We get it from being told that countless people are better than we are. We get it from parents who want us to be a certain way, teachers who fail us when we don't fit into the cookie cutout of what it means to be educated, religious leaders who claim we are born sinners, magazines that show we aren't sexy enough, celebrities who bring home to us that we don't have enough money, and advertisers who tell us we will never have enough stuff. We are constantly being bombarded with the message that who we are and what we have are not good enough, but I'm here to tell you it's time to stop listening to such nonsense and way past time to stop believing it. You don't need to be fixed, and you definitely don't need more stuff in order to be truly happy. You already have everything you need right now in this very moment to be at ease with your life and yourself.

Another issue with the idea of self-improvement is that it tends to overemphasize the future. This means the "better" person you hope to become is not here now but rather in some future moment when you've finally been able to get rid of all the junk you don't like about yourself and the life you're currently living. But here's the fine print: this imagined time and place where everything is complete and as it "should be" will never be *now* and will always be beyond your reach. In fact, this endless yearning for the "future you" robs you of the deeper joy and contentment that comes from jumping right into the raw and beautiful disaster you're trying so desperately to change. Is it possible that your own desire to become something other than what you already are is causing you the very suffering you're hoping to escape?

The fact of the matter is, happiness and suffering are both conditional. Conditional happiness arises based on certain causes and conditions, stays around for a while, and then ceases to be—always. And suffering is like this too: suffering arises based on certain causes and conditions, stays around for a while, and then ceases to be. You can't hold on to happiness, nor can you permanently escape from suffering. It is the nature of things to fall apart, and even if you do finally manage to get it all together, life will inevitably change and your temporary perfection will be nothing more than a memory. You may find this message pessimistic, but if you allow it to take root in your heart, you'll find it's actually a realistic breath of fresh air. It's actually very good news indeed.

You can spend the rest of your days attempting to become some imagined, perfect person, but I recommend you don't waste your life striving to become some unattainable version of yourself. You'll never reach the place of perfection, and that's perfectly all right. The path to perfection will lead only to exhaustion and disappointment; meanwhile, your actual life will be passing you by. The more peaceful and practical approach is simply to be yourself every moment, accept that this being human is a messy ordeal, and learn to be okay with getting your hands dirty, so to speak. There's no actual happiness to be found in always trying to be someone else at some future time, because the fact is, you'll never quite get there. Why not, instead, show up fully, right here, right now? Allow yourself to let go of the idea that who you already are isn't enough and realize this deep acceptance is the path to real freedom.

2
IS HAPPINESS REALLY A WARM PUPPY?

My life has no purpose, no direction, no aim, no meaning, and yet I'm happy. I can't figure it out. What am I doing right?
—CHARLES M. SCHULZ

ALL OF US are just trying to be happy. Whether it's striving to get good grades in school, planning vacations, or seeking out love and affection—you name it—as individuals, societies, and even as a species, we've tried it all. Chasing pleasure and security while avoiding discomfort and uncertainty may seem like a logical path to happiness—but it's not one that actually exists. Can't be done. Moreover, if you honestly look into your life, has this approach ever brought you lasting fulfillment or peace of mind? If it were really that simple, we would all be happy already, and pharmaceutical companies would be going bankrupt as people stopped filling prescriptions for anxiety and depression. Clearly, this is not the case.

So . . . what is this thing called happiness? For most, it is the pursuit of pleasurable feelings and favorable situations. However you may describe it, one thing is always true: happiness is fleeting and temporary at best—and leaves a constant craving for more. I think you know what I'm talking about. Once the initial "warm puppy" feelings start to wane, you want more. What people don't realize is that this *pursuit of happiness* is profoundly flawed—it keeps you trapped in a cycle of suffering. You want happiness, you chase after it, you get it, you fear losing it, you ultimately *do* lose it, and then you try desperately to re-create it. Sound familiar? If not, start looking harder. By constantly pursuing happiness, we never quite get hold of it.

Albert Einstein famously defined insanity as doing the same thing over and over again while expecting different results. This endless pursuit of happiness over suffering is what we have been doing constantly for as long as we have been alive—if not longer. How's it worked out for you? Not so good, right? Don't you think it's time you take a different approach?

Let us consider a more practical definition of happiness. Simply put, happiness is contentment—the peace of mind that comes from opening up to and fully accepting your life right here and now. It's not a feeling, it's deeper than that, and it has absolutely nothing to do with having things go according to *your* plan. This form of happiness is not gained from having a certain kind of experience but, rather, is how you relate to everything you experience. In the words of the Vietnamese Zen master Thich Nhat Hanh, "There is no way to happiness—happiness is the way." This means whether you are feeling on top of the world or crushed by its weight, you have the power to fully accept yourself and your life just the way it is, and with practice, you'll come to find happiness is *always* a possibility—but only when it's understood correctly. Stop struggling, resisting, and running from what is, and you will find an inner peace beyond all material conditions awaiting you.

This is actual happiness, and the good news is that it's available in your life right now.

3
THE PRESENT MOMENT

To live in the present moment is a miracle. The miracle is not to walk on water. The miracle is to walk on the green Earth in the present moment, to appreciate the peace and beauty that are available now.
—THICH NHAT HANH

THERE'S A BUDDHIST STORY about a woman who decided she wanted to become enlightened. She asked all the various spiritual teachers in the area what the best way was to do this. They advised her to climb up the highest mountain and go deep into the cave located at its peak. She was told she would find a wise old woman in the cave who could help her find enlightenment. She went on her journey, and after much hardship she finally reached the cave, where, sure enough, she found a little old woman sitting in meditation. She bowed to the wise woman and explained her quest, asking her if she could help her attain realization. The old woman smiled and asked the seeker if she was sure that's what she wanted. Of course she answered *yes*, whereupon the old woman turned into a demon with a stick and began chasing her, screaming, "Now, now, now!" For the rest of her days, the woman could never escape that shouting demon.

Strange as it may seem, this story shows how the key to enlightenment is found in precise and consistent awareness of the present moment. Although this book isn't necessarily aimed at Buddhist enlightenment, what I've been calling actual happiness can also be found only in the present moment. This means that right now, whoever you are, whatever thoughts and feelings you are experiencing, whatever life situation you may be in—these are the perfect conditions for peace and happiness. Yes, I said *the perfect conditions*. In fact, there really is no other place where you can be. The past has already . . . well . . . passed, and the future hasn't yet manifested. That leaves you with only one possibility: the here and now.

But what is it about *now* that is so liberating? What does the present moment have to do with actual happiness? Many spiritual teachers and practitioners, including myself, are always talking about being present in the moment. So what's the big deal? What's all of this fuss about the present moment, and why is it useful to be there?

The present moment is the only place you can actually live your life. It's where you can speak, where you can act, where you can help others, and where you can choose to not be stuck in limiting thoughts, reactive emotions, or destructive habits. The problem is we have a mind that creates a past, a future, and an endless supply of story lines and judgments. To make things worse, we hold on to these false realities as the one and only truth of reality.

How much time do *you* spend reliving memories of the past? "If only I had done it this way." "If only things had gone like this instead of that." *If only, if only, if only.* It seems as though we believe that by repeatedly sorting out and rethinking our memories, this will somehow change the way things happened and magically make our present situation different. My advice is to give up all hope for a better past and learn to see the absurdity of endlessly trying to bring it back to life. Realize that actual happiness cannot be found in what's been—because it's over with and no longer exists—but, rather, is found in the freshness of *this* moment.

The future, on the other hand, is also a terrible place to seek peace.

For many of us, the search for future happiness begins with the desire to get good grades and an education. "Once I graduate from high school, I'll be happy." But then comes college. "If only I could get into the college I like, then I'll be happy." You get into college but still aren't happy because then comes graduating, followed by finding a job, looking for a partner, buying a house, starting a family, and so forth. Do you notice the pattern? As soon as you get what you want, you find yourself looking toward what's next. The future promise of peace and fulfillment never comes because there is always something next to be achieved or overcome. There's always more; it never ends.

It's clear that the past and the future have no way to bring you the fulfillment you desire. Neither truly exists except in your mind as memories or anticipations. As you investigate this, you will find that *right now* is the only moment you have. *This moment* is where everything happens. Fully engaging in this very moment, no matter what may be present, is fully living in the reality of your life. Find peace right here—it's your only option. There is no other time and no other place.

Don't be one of the walking dead, unconsciously living your life in your mind through memories and anticipations. Life is passing you by right now—and there may not be a tomorrow. Open up to your life right now and make peace with it, and whether you're full of smiles or full of frowns, experience it fully.

4
THE THREE MARKS OF EXISTENCE

The time has come to think more wisely, hasn't it?

—Tenzin Gyatso,
The Fourteenth Dalai Lama

THERE'S AN OLD JOKE about a person looking for inner peace going to see a meditation master.

"I want peace. How do I get it?" asks the seeker.

"Well," says the master. "First remove the *I*, as this is the ego. Then remove the *want*, as this is desire. What's left?"

Easier said than done, though!

If you'd like to find peace and contentment in your life, you first need to understand the nature of both yourself and your desires. You must also be clear as to what can and cannot fulfill you. There's a Buddhist teaching called the *three marks of existence* that is helpful for clarifying this.

Over twenty-five hundred years ago the Buddha taught that all phenomena in the entire universe are "marked" with three characteristics:

- Impermanence
- Suffering/unsatisfactoriness
- Selflessness

In essence, what this teaching points to is this: All phenomena—from thoughts, feelings, and emotions to people, places, and things—are always in a constant state of change; this is the great flow of the universe. Because everything is in this continuous cycle of change, nothing in the world is able to bring you full satisfaction but only short moments of temporary fulfillment. This leads to a constant state of what Buddhists call *dukkha*, which is often translated as "suffering" or "dissatisfaction" or "unsatisfactoriness."

In other words, all the things that you think might bring happiness provide only temporary satisfaction, leaving you constantly craving more. Lastly, selflessness—not to be confused with the opposite of being selfish—shows who you think you are is only an illusion, as you too are always in a constant state of flux. Given that there is nothing permanent to be found anywhere in an impermanent universe, even the concept of an unchanging, separate self cannot endure. Without recognizing and accepting that these three phenomena exist, you will undoubtedly continue to struggle in your attempt to attain peace.

Let's look at these three marks in a little more detail.

IMPERMANENCE

That nothing is static or fixed, that all is fleeting and impermanent, is the first mark of existence. It is the ordinary state of affairs. Everything is in process.

Everything—every tree, every blade of grass, all the animals, insects, human beings, buildings, the animate and the

> *inanimate—is always changing, moment to moment.*
>
> —PEMA CHÖDRÖN

I once heard a story about a king who, in trying to teach one of his servants humility, told him to find a ring that when worn was able to make the happy sad and the unhappy glad. Knowing that no such ring existed, he sent the servant off, giving him six months to seek it. The servant searched all over the land to no avail. The night before the six months expired, he met a wise man in a village and asked, "Do you know of a ring that when worn can make the happy sad and the unhappy glad?" The wise man silently nodded his head and engraved a few words on a ring. The following day the king summoned the servant and asked if he had found the ring. While everyone in the room, including the king, was getting ready to laugh and humiliate him, the servant handed him the ring. The cheerful mood of the king changed as he read the words engraved on it: This Too Shall Pass.

Obviously, this short fable illustrates the first of the three marks of existence: impermanence. Impermanence is the only unchanging promise life has to offer. Everything in the entire universe is in a constant state of movement. Whether it's thoughts and sensations or people and situations, nothing can escape this truth. Impermanence is everywhere, and it's here to stay. Truly understanding impermanence allows you to be more fluid when things in your life change, and it can also remind you to cherish and be grateful for that which you already have in your life.

Accepting impermanence can be a frightening ordeal, and although it's around you all the time, it's usually uncomfortable when changes occur, as it leaves no ground to stand on. Nothing can be grasped or truly owned. If you try holding on to pleasurable feelings, experiences, or emotions, you'll quickly realize that this is an impossible task. For example, imagine you just bought a new iPhone. You are filled with joy and excitement—you finally have the phone you have been waiting for! You download all the new apps available and immediately begin using its cool new features. The excitement quickly wears off though, and after only a few weeks (at most!), this once wonderful phone will just be your plain old phone again. On top of this, you find out that in a few months the newer, better version of the phone will be released. Now the phone that brought you such joy and excitement seems outdated and useless in comparison with the new one. The iPhone you own is now a constant reminder of what you don't have. Bummer, dude!

Impermanence can become a major source of anxiety in your life. It's this underlying uneasiness that drives your mind to create the idea of a permanent self that holds tightly to beliefs, thoughts, and emotions. If you deny or resist impermanence, you will cause a significant amount of unnecessary suffering—but it doesn't have to be this way. You don't need to resist change. You only need to let things through, let them be, and let them go, riding the changes of your life like a leaf floating down a stream. Change will happen whether you like it or not—sometimes for better and other times for worse. Once you understand and make peace with it, things become workable; you can stop resisting and instead learn to just go with it. As I tell my yoga students during class all the time, "You can either drown in the ocean of life, or you can learn how to surf."

There's a story I read of meditation master Ajahn Chah, who was asked how he could be so happy in an impermanent world. In response, he held up his favorite cup—a gift given to him by a friend—and told the questioners how much he enjoyed this cup. He said he especially enjoyed how it held water splendidly, shimmered in the sunlight, and made a beautiful ringing sound when he tapped it. He then said that although one day it may break, he would still enjoy it while it's intact, fully knowing its nature is to fall apart.

Ajahn Chah was pointing out the truth of impermanence. All things, including you, are temporarily together. Like everything in the entire universe, you are already "broken," or to put it differently, you are a transitory combination of various elements. The only fate for your body and mind, and for all other things in your life, is to fall apart or to break. This can be quite a heavy realization, but instead of feeling upset about this, you can actually use it to increase the peace and joy in your life. I think Steve Jobs, the American entrepreneur and past CEO of Apple Inc., understood this when he said that remembering that you are going to die is the best way to avoid the trap of thinking you have something to lose.

Accepting the nature of impermanence can be a useful tool when dealing with your thoughts and emotions. Realizing that anger is a transient state of mind, instead of completely losing it when you're upset, you can let it pass—naturally and of its own accord. Although it's uncomfortable to be pissed off, once you remember that it, like all things, will pass, it's much easier to not chew out the person who keeps pushing your buttons. If you understand impermanence and are having worrisome thoughts, you will know how your thoughts pass through your mind like clouds in the sky, and you can let them go rather than become ensnared and controlled by them. If you are feeling pain due to an illness or disease, you can carefully observe the pain from a place of acceptance, watching how it changes form from one moment to the next. This will create the space needed in your mind to let it be there, freeing you from the pain and suffering of feeling like a victim.

Being able to recognize impermanence is also liberating when experiencing pleasure. Knowing that happiness and pleasurable feelings and sensations are based on changing conditions, you can be grateful for any moment you experience them. Spending time with those you care about will be even more special by acknowledging impermanence; the fact that this person will not be around forever will allow you to appreciate every second in their company.

Impermanence is around you all the time and can be very liberating once you begin opening up to and relaxing into it. One good practice is to try noticing impermanence in all things through-out your daily routine. Take a look around and see how everything, even you, is in a constant state of change. Appointments come and go, as do feelings, thoughts, and people. Every moment is a new moment because nothing is solid and nothing goes unchanged. Impermanence can be a blessing if you are feeling down or having a bad day. Just remind yourself that "this too shall pass," and encourage yourself to stay with these emotions or situations until they have passed. You can also try using this truth to help you cher-ish each and every happy moment of your life, because these too are fleeting.

The bottom line is this: you don't need to try to escape from difficult feelings, people, or situa-tions. Change will happen on its own, and there's no need to run from it once it does. In fact, you can learn to find immense gratitude and joy through embracing change and appreciating the beauty found in life's ever-changing dance. Simply go with the flow—one breath and one step at a time—and see for yourself, with welcoming arms, where life takes you.

SUFFERING

I teach one thing and one thing only: suffering and the end of suffering.
—THE BUDDHA

Suffering is the second of the three marks of existence. It is an inescapable part of life that comes in many forms, such as physical pain and discomfort, mental anguish, cravings, and desires. Whether you like it or not (and presumably you don't), suffering pervades your life each and every day. Well . . . that sounds awfully pessimistic, but don't worry—there's hope.

Normally when you think of the word *suffering*, you think of extreme pain, torture, and agony. Although this is a form of suffering that exists, it is not the kind I am talking about here. A more fitting definition for the suffering I am referring to is discomfort, dissatisfaction, or uneasiness. This is the basic restlessness and anxiety that are at the core of your being and the result of living in an impermanent world. Because all things are constantly changing, there is nothing to permanently hold on to or own. Whether it's your house, job, family, or friends, or even your body, emotions, or thoughts, nothing stays the same or lasts forever. This constant state of movement leaves you in an uneasy, groundless state, which shakes you to the core and creates an underlying discomfort that you just can't seem to shake off.

From this primordial uneasiness comes a desire for permanence—for some solid, unchanging ground to walk on. By constantly trying to ground yourself in a world that's naturally groundless, you end up clinging tightly to belief systems, judgments, ideas, and ways of being that keep you feeling comfortable and secure. Of course, all of these are also impermanent, so the comfort and security you feel is only a temporary illusion, which if provoked, can escalate quickly into aggression.

An extreme version of this desire for security can be found with fundamentalists of any kind. Many people become very aggressive when someone is poking holes in their security blanket, whether related to political beliefs or religious views. If you honestly think about it, we are all fundamentalists, because we are always solidifying our views about things, people, and places. We also solidify our beliefs about ourselves, the way we see family members and friends, how we believe we should look or act, the way we think life should be, and so on. As soon as these ideas are challenged or shattered, your safe and secure world falls apart, leaving you uncomfortable in a place of uncertainty. Don't believe me? The next time someone challenges one of your opinions or views, notice how quickly and righteously you solidify yourself.

Inevitable Suffering vs. Added Suffering

In order to be at peace with yourself and your life just the way it is, you must be able to see clearly what causes additional suffering to you and those around you, then begin to stop the causes from which it arises. With some kinds of suffering, this is possible; with others, it's not exactly. This is because there are in fact two main types of suffering: inevitable suffering and added suffering.

Inevitable suffering is the pain and discomfort that are an unavoidable part of life. It includes both physical and emotional pain, as well as the fact of impermanence and the fact that all of this will eventually come to an end. Added suffering is the suffering created in your mind, which you grab hold of and attach to your life. This type of suffering is optional, avoidable, and unnecessary and can amplify and extend the inevitable suffering.

Inevitable suffering comes in the form of physical and emotional pain. Physical pain can be avoided for only so long. Even if you could somehow prevent breaking a bone, getting your wisdom teeth pulled, twisting your ankle, stubbing your toe, burning your tongue on a hot cup of coffee, or any other accident that can cause physical pain, you still couldn't hide from pain forever. As your body ages, it will naturally continue to break down, become weaker, and eventually stop functioning altogether. Aging, sickness, and death are painful aspects of life that none of us can escape.

There are also certain emotional pains that simply come with the territory of being human (e.g., the grief from losing a loved one, the heartbreak of a broken relationship, and the fear of death, dying, and the unknown). The human mind has evolved to be a certain way, unavoidably reacting emotionally to various circumstances and situations. This is nothing to worry about, as it is as natural as the changing of the seasons, but it is something that is present in your life and needs to be respected, thoroughly investigated, and clearly understood—not as things to take personally but, rather, as passing events floating through your awareness.

Added suffering, on the other hand, is the suffering your mind throws on top of your inevitable suffering—a sort of commentary on your direct experience of sensations and feelings. This type of suffering can be found in your thoughts, fantasies, anticipations, and the underlying story lines you tell yourself on a daily basis. For example, let's say your significant other has cheated on you. The pain of heartbreak you will feel is the inevitable suffering. Nevertheless, as uncomfortable as it may be, it will pass naturally with time. Added suffering is all the thoughts that follow this emotional reaction to the situation: "What's wrong with me?" "No one will ever love me." "I am unlovable." Added suffering arises when you are unable to stay with the underlying, impermanent, painful feelings of a situation and instead grasp on to the beliefs and thoughts of your mind.

This will continually renew the painful feelings rather than allow them to flow through naturally.

Added suffering can also be associated with pleasant feelings and experiences. These come in the form of cravings, desires, and addictions. One extreme example is an addiction to drugs. Let's just say that one time you decided to try a drug and had the most wonderful experience. You swallowed one tiny pill, and all your worries vanished and your entire body was full of bliss. A few hours later, though, the high wore off, and you returned to feeling like your plain old shitty, foolish self. The problem is that your mind continually craves that experience over and over, since the high was so good. Mind you, you were fine and at peace until the craving came and disturbed it, but now you think the only way back to peace is through fulfilling this craving. And this is how the cycle of added suffering begins.

Subtler forms of these cravings or desires can be seen with eating, exercising, certain ways of acting around others, or anything that makes you feel pleasure. But just to be clear: the arising of desires is, in and of itself, not a problem, but as you habituate yourself to following them, you may find that you are craving the pleasurable reward more and more, entrapping yourself in a prison of desires. Through constantly chasing pleasure and security, you run yourself around in circles, seeking a permanent satisfaction that will never come. Because of this your mind is never at rest, and peace is not a possibility.

With practice you can notice cravings and desires as just thoughts, or impersonal events in the mind, and let them come and go as they please. There's no need to get rid of anything, and nothing needs to be fixed. Try this: Next time you have an intense craving for something, instead of feeding it—by doing exactly what it's telling you to do—try sitting down with it. Get to know it. What is the feeling tone of this craving? Where is it felt in your body? Will the world really fall apart if you don't do what it's asking? Are you willing to find out? Become curious about it, and through deep investigation and reflection, find out its true nature. You may be surprised with what you uncover.

It's clear that there is some suffering you cannot avoid. This inevitable suffering is part of being human and should be expected, but the added suffering is a kind of choice we make in every moment to either grasp on to the endless chatter of our minds or live free of their limiting views and perceptions. Why choose to add more suffering to something that's already painful to begin with? It's like getting shot with an arrow, but instead of pulling it out and tending to the wound, you take more arrows and begin shooting yourself in the same spot again . . . and again . . . and again.

But there's an alternative to this madness. Start accepting the inevitable suffering in your life, understanding that things always change, and practice not piling extra suffering on top of it—even if you can only do it in little ways at first. Do your best to make friends with whatever you are feeling so that you won't try to run away from pain when it arises or endlessly follow cravings for pleasure. Otherwise, peace will never be a possibility.

The Benefits of Suffering

There is an old Buddhist story of a woman whose only child passes away. Desperate for answers and someone to help her, she is led to the Buddha. He tells her that he can revive her child, but first she must go around her village and receive a mustard seed from a house where no one has experienced the loss of a family member. Anxious to bring back her child, she goes off into the village searching for houses that have not experienced suffering from the death of a loved one. Of course, she returns to the Buddha empty-handed. The woman then realizes that the Buddha was teaching her that everyone in her village has undergone the suffering she was experiencing, and although it did not relieve the unavoidable pain from her loss, it took her from a limited view of "*my* suffering" to the truth of "there is suffering." Put another way, she saw how her pain was not hers alone but, rather, a shared universal experience of loss from which none of us can escape.

Like the woman in the story, most of us do not want to experience the suffering in our lives. But whether we like it or not, it is part of "the whole catastrophe," as Zorba the Greek would call it. Rather than complaining about it or trying to avoid it, you can extract great benefits from the suffering you encounter in your life. By simply understanding that suffering exists—while changing your attitude toward it—you will find that suffering can be used as the fertilizer to cultivate humbleness, compassion, and understanding.

Suffering has the ability to knock down the walls of ignorance you have created. For example, when a tragic event such as loss or disease happens in your life, the world as you know it will be shattered. No matter how much money you have or how important you are at your job or in society, you will still experience suffering just the same. The suffering from these events has the ability to soften your way of being and connect you with the penetrating sadness of life. If you allow it, this sadness will leave you less self-centered, removing both pride and arrogance.

Suffering also cultivates compassion. When you suffer, you understand that your suffering is shared with all people. Realizing your shared suffering allows you to empathize with others who are going through similar experiences. This can shift your perspective from the smallness of only *you* suffering to the simple fact that suffering exists everywhere. Once you awaken to this truth, you will find that every time you suffer, your heart will ache for the billions of other people experiencing the same thing, and with that ache you are connected to them. Ultimately, this becomes a form of compassion.

Lastly, suffering allows you to understand and properly deal with the workings of karma. We'll look at it in more detail in the next chapter, but in brief, karma is the law of cause and effect. This means that every thought, action, and word is creating your future. Once you see life clearly, through mindfulness and meditation, you will learn what leads to more suffering and what leads to less. You will be able to use your suffering to see what does and does not work, and you will learn to plant seeds that cultivate less suffering in the future for both you and others.

SELFLESSNESS

A human being is part of a whole, called by us the Universe, a part limited in time and space. He experiences himself, his thoughts and feelings, as something separated from the rest, a kind of optical delusion of his consciousness. This delusion is a kind of prison for us, restricting us to our personal desires and to affection for a few persons nearest us. Our

task must be to free ourselves from this
prison by widening our circles of compas-
sion to embrace all living creatures and
the whole of nature in its beauty.
—ALBERT EINSTEIN

The third mark of existence is selflessness, and although it may seem a little abstract at first— it's some pretty deep stuff—I will do my best to explain. It's normal for you to think that you are a solid, unchanging, and separate self—and perhaps it feels to you that this "self" is located somewhere between your eyes and ears. With this concept being so common and familiar, the idea that you are not the way you think you are wouldn't even cross your mind—especially since you're associating this sense of *I* with the mind and body. You probably believe that you are your body. If you were the body, then if any part of it were lost, part of you would disappear along with it. This is obviously not the case. Not only do you cut your hair and nails often, with no loss of "self," but every cell in your body is constantly renewing itself. Additionally, many people have had organs replaced with no changes to their sense of self.

There are so many processes happening each moment for you to be here, besides what you are consciously aware of. Usually you associate *I* only with the conscious, voluntary actions of your body, as "you" have never intentionally beat your own heart, digested your own food, or made your fingernails grow. How could the self be some parts of your body but not all parts? If you are not controlling the unconscious, involuntary aspects of your body, then who or what is? With no clear answer it may be tempting to believe that you yourself must be found in your thoughts and emotions. You can observe both, but if you were only these, then you, too, would disappear once they passed. In addition, there would also have to be two selves, because one thing can't observe itself any more than a tooth can bite itself. Furthermore, upon observing your mind, you will notice the chaotic, uncontrollable nature of mental activity that arises. Your thoughts come out of nowhere and go back to nowhere, yet the feeling that you are there is present throughout. On rare occasions, there may even be no thoughts at all in your mind. Where is this sense of self during these moments? Where can you be found, if not in your thoughts, emotions, or body? Who are you really? Where are you *really* located in your body and mind? The Buddhist tradition holds up the assertion that no matter how much you search, you will never find a fixed self.

Another aspect of selflessness is a Buddhist concept called dependent co-arising. This points to the fact that everything in the universe is produced by prior causes and conditions. For example, a tree is not a solid and separate entity but, rather, a result coming from many different causes and conditions, including a seed, dirt, water, earth, the sun, the universe, all the way back to any and every cause and condition throughout all of beginningless time prior to and during the tree's existence. Likewise, you come from and depend on an infinite amount of causes and conditions. Without your parents (and their parents, and their parents, etc.), you would not exist; without the perfect conditions of Earth, life would not exist; without the universe, Earth would not exist, and on and on and on. . . .

All things throughout the entire universe are interdependent and lack a solid and separate identity. Everything depends on everything else for its own existence; therefore, separation from the whole universe can be nothing more than a temporary illusion. In order to understand this, imagine a triangle—three straight lines on a blank piece of paper. A straight line alone is not a triangle, nor can any sense of triangularity be found on a blank piece of paper. The triangle arises only when the three straight lines form together in a certain way on the blank piece of paper. Clearly the triangle does not exist without the lines or the piece of paper, yet neither of these is the triangle itself. So where is the triangle? It is nowhere to be found; hence, it is empty of an existence separate from those three lines and the paper on which they're drawn.

Or think about a car. A car is made up of a variety of parts and materials, each of which, when separated, clearly is not a car. The steering wheel is not the car. The wheels are not the car. The motor is not the car. . . . It's only when these separate parts are joined together in a certain way that a temporary "car-ness" appears. You can view yourself similarly by recognizing the many causes and conditions that you never considered yourself to be, including food, water, oxygen, trees, and so on.

All of these allow you to exist, yet they never have been called part of you. But how can they not be? By observing the interrelation of your own body—including your thoughts and emotions—with the external environment, you will find that dependent co-arising is always at work. In a sense, then, we could say that all things are boundless because everything depends on everything else to exist, leaving us with one interrelated, ever-changing phenomenon, which is life in the here and now.

Just to clarify, selflessness does not mean that you are nothing, like an empty void; rather, selflessness is the fact that you are not as solid and separate from the rest of the world as you may think. Perhaps we could replace the word *selflessness* with *interdependence*, as there are no boundaries that separate you from anything else, making you completely interdependent with all of your experience. Understanding your interdependence, and knowing that you are not limited only to your thoughts, feelings, and sensations, can be a liberating realization—it just might allow you to take yourself less seriously.

You'll find that there is nothing you have to change or get rid of. Remember, change happens naturally all by itself. The emotions and thoughts you experience, whether positive or negative, are nothing more than passing phenomena—energy moving and changing, interacting and relating to the world around you. Don't let this limit how and who you are. Remember that you don't have to try so hard to discard or remove these thoughts and emotions, they will come and go on their own; rather, you must practice getting yourself unstuck from their seductive grips. Realizing and aligning with the third mark of existence, selflessness, gives you this freedom.

Embracing the three marks of existence is necessary in order to experience actual happiness in this lifetime. In fact, it seems to me to be the most practical way to live. This is because the three marks of existence all point toward actual truths about your life. If your life is marked with these three characteristics, don't you think you ought to align yourself with them? How much unnecessary suffering could be released if you truly understood them? I hope you will investigate this and find out for yourself.

5
HOW TO USE SUFFERING TO CULTIVATE COMPASSION

When we honor the gate of suffering, what arises is the wondrous power of compassion.

—Jack Kornfield

THE BUDDHA TAUGHT that suffering was an inevitable part of being human. He wasn't trying to be pessimistic, or to say that all of life is miserable, but instead was pointing to a simple fact of our existence. Everybody suffers. It isn't that God is punishing us, or that we have done something wrong, but simply that we are alive in an impermanent world. Of course there will be suffering! Understanding this truth allows us to stop resisting and struggling with the ever-changing, oftentimes uncomfortable, nature of our lives. Unfortunately, this is easier said than done and practice is often needed.

Embracing your suffering and the suffering of all beings can bring you to a tender space within yourself—but like most of us, you may find yourself running away as soon as you feel the rawness of this vulnerability. Usually, the armor goes up and your heart becomes hardened, but it is possible to let go of your habitual ways of escaping your difficulties and, instead, learn to relax and open to your suffering in a way that can bring you peace while also cultivating compassion.

There are many wonderful Buddhist practices that help cultivate compassion in the face of suffering—and don't worry, you don't need to convert to Buddhism to put them into practice. The simplest, most effective approach I have found is a three-step method taught by the Buddhist nun Pema Chödrön. You start this practice by first acknowledging the suffering you are feeling.

Then you recognize nonjudgmentally how hard it is to experience it, and lastly, you wish that you and all beings experiencing this type of suffering be free from it.

For example, if you are having overwhelming anxiety one morning, you start this practice by coming fully into the moment. Bring your hand to your heart and for a moment experience the texture of the anxiety in your body. Where do you feel it? Is it sharp or dull? Hot or cool? Hold the feeling in your awareness and see what it really feels like. Also, notice the thoughts accompanying the feelings. What are they saying to you? Is it the whole truth? Do you believe the thoughts? Once you have directly experienced the state of your body and mind, you can begin to acknowledge how hard it is for you to feel this way. This is building self-compassion.

In a nonjudgmental way, simply express how hard it is to be feeling the way you feel. "Having anxiety is a real struggle for me," is a good example of acknowledging that you are having a hard time with it but not judging it as bad, or wrong. You are not saying, "I hate this stupid anxiety," or "I can't stand feeling this way." Rather, you are simply reflecting honestly what's happening in the present moment. Lastly, you extend freedom from the anxiety to yourself and to all other people suffering from it. You may say something like this, "May all beings, including me, be free from the suffering of anxiety." Of course this doesn't actually free people from their suffering, but it trains your mind to use your suffering as a way to cultivate compassion and allows you to move closer to the discomforts and pains you'd normally want to run away from.

Approaching your suffering in this way allows it to become a tool to cultivate compassion. Your suffering can be transformed, and your heart can become expansive enough to hold any difficult times you may experience. Through the depths of your suffering, compassion can shine brightly.

I recently had a personal experience of suffering involving my grandfather that led to much love and compassion throughout my entire family and me.

My grandfather had been battling bladder cancer for almost ten years. He underwent many treatments, keeping the cancer at bay, but only this past year when it returned yet again did they finally decide to completely remove his bladder. Although he was seventy-nine years old at the time, the surgery went exceedingly well, and his recovery was even better. He was quickly up and moving around, and snapped right back to his old self in no time. He had to make a few adjustments, of course, but nothing he couldn't handle. Things were looking good.

Unfortunately, the next phase of the treatment was chemotherapy, as tests had shown the cancer had spread beyond the bladder. He scheduled his appointment and did his treatment. Everything seemed fine for a few days, until the side-effects began. The chemo made him so sick he had to be admitted to the hospital, where he unfortunately remained for many weeks.

With each visit, he seemed to be deteriorating more and more. He lost a lot of weight, along with his hair, and eventually, started losing cognitive abilities. I remember one night I canceled work to stay with him because I truly believed he was going to pass away within a few hours. He was going in and out of consciousness, continually lifting his arm up and down, seemingly out of his control, and quietly moaned and cursed in pain, although when we asked him if anything was hurting, he said he felt fine. It was a scary, heartbreaking time.

Although there was great suffering and pain among the entire family, the amount of love expressed and felt was immense. It seemed as though the usual family dramas had quieted down, and everyone seemed much more present and gentle. Hugs were longer and talks were deeper. Everyone in the family would visit often, bringing my grandfather tasty treats, gifts, and heartfelt cards. Everyone also helped my grandmother while my grandfather was immobilized and stuck in the hospital bed. It was both horrible and special all at the same time.

Suffering can indeed be unpleasant and sometimes cause us to close our hearts, making us bitter and cold. But if you allow it to penetrate your being, it can actually bring you to the tender and vulnerable realm of the heart. When experienced from the heart, suffering can blossom into loving-kindness, compassion, gratitude, peace, and even joy. I know this to be true for me— during this dark time with my grandfather, all I remember was feeling immense love for him and for my entire family. I wanted to be there and I wanted to help relieve *everyone's* suffering.

I believe the true nature of our being is good, and painful events such as illnesses, accidents, or even deaths create a groundlessness that, if allowed, can quiet the self-centered ego mind, leading you straight to the heart. From the tender open heart of sadness, compassion flows through you like a river and envelops all you come in contact with.

6
KARMA

If you want to know your past, look into your present conditions. If you want to know your future, look into your present actions.

—Chinese proverb

Much of your practice is finding new ways of dealing with your own personal karma. What is karma, though? *Karma* literally translates to "action," and as you remember from high school physics, *"every action has an equal and opposite reaction."* In other words, there are consequences to every action, which may bring pleasant, unpleasant, or neutral results. Sometimes the consequences are immediate. Other times, the consequences take months or even years to bear their fruit. For example, if you punch a wall you immediately feel pain. Instant karma! On the other hand, if you continue to speak ill of someone, the negative results of that may be harder to see, or slower to be apparent—but they're real nonetheless.

Please note: I am not talking about some airy-fairy idea of karma where there is someone judging your behavior, giving out punishments or rewards depending on what you're doing. Instead, I'm simply pointing you to the fact that everything you think, speak, or do will have consequences that will someday need to be faced.

Imagine every thought you think, every word you speak, and every action you take as little seeds in a big garden. Your whole life you have been continually planting seeds, experiencing the fruits of these seeds, and planting more seeds in reaction to what has grown. Each seed will grow, and eventually the fruit of our actions must be faced. Take a moment and reflect on your life up to this point. What kinds of seeds have you been planting? What type of garden will you be expecting?

Look first at what you have been thinking. From your mind, all words and actions are born.

You may believe your thoughts can't possibly have any consequences, especially since you're the only one aware of them. If you don't like a coworker but you keep that thought to yourself, what's the big deal? The big deal is that thoughts eventually become words and/or actions. Ultimately, repeated thought patterns will either be spoken or acted upon. And even if you somehow manage to not speak it or act it out, people can still sense what's going on in your head by your body language. Just think of the last time you were around someone who didn't like you very much. Couldn't you feel the dislike radiating off of them? Didn't it make you uncomfortable?

When it comes to your thoughts and emotions, you can understand karma as a *tendency* to be a certain way. Karma doesn't have to be a fate that binds you but, rather, can be something that is noticed, worked with, and released. Throughout this book, I'll point to ways that will help you be better able to observe the habits in your mind, giving you the freedom to go beyond the karmic tendencies you have created. By simply observing the mind, you are creating space rather than continually and ignorantly going in the same direction.

Try looking at how you speak, both to yourself and to others. Is it kind or judgmental? Do you speak to people with an open, receptive mind, truly listening to what they are saying, or do you come filled with opinions, caring only about what you want to say? Do your words uplift people and help them see their potential, or do they put them down? Words have the potential to transform a person or completely destroy them. Contemplate how you've been speaking, internally and externally. What will your future be like if you continue speaking this way? Have you been choosing your words wisely?

Lastly, take a good hard look at what you *do*. What do you do for a living? Is it bringing harm to people or the environment? Or is it truly helping others? Are you acting habitually, or freely? Which actions are causing harm to you and those around you? Why do you continue to act in this way? Can you let go of these ways of acting? Which actions are beneficial to you and others? How can you cultivate these more?

If you plant an apple tree, you will get apples. If you plant a lemon tree, you will get lemons. You cannot plant an apple tree and get lemons, and vice versa. The same is true with your own karma garden. If you act, speak, or think unwholesomely, you cannot expect wholesome results. It just doesn't work that way. Selfishness, greed, and hatred lead to suffering. Only compassion, gentleness, and kindness can give you wholesome results.

If you want to suffer less and experience actual happiness, look at what you're thinking, saying, and doing. Most of the unnecessary, added suffering in your life is a result of not paying much attention to these three things. This is why Buddhist practice, and other religions, start off by teaching ethics and morality, because a lot of suffering could be avoided if you just thought, spoke, and acted with awareness, discernment, and compassion.

Start off your day understanding that everything you do today is planting seeds for tomorrow, and then end your day looking back at how the day went and see if there is any place you could put more effort into. Recognize that what you experience right now is the fruit of past experiences. How you deal with this moment will plant more seeds for your future. Also remember, becoming a little bit nicer, or changing what you do one time, will not magically erase years of doing the opposite. Again, your present condition is the result of what you've done, a sum total of all the past choices you've made, and how you deal with that right now is creating your future. The present moment is full of both cause and result, and how you relate to that is going to affect the next moment, so choose wisely.

Being your shitty, foolish self doesn't mean you can't do anything or that you're helpless and your life is a hopeless waste that will never change; rather, it's about accepting where you are and not being so hard on yourself as you work with and through your own personal karma. If you want a more peaceful future, start right now by observing yourself. Use the mindfulness and meditation practices found later in this book to determine which thoughts, actions, and words will bring about less suffering in your life and in the lives around you, and try cultivating those seeds. The "shitty" characteristics of your person- ality do not need to be changed or suppressed in any way—they only need to be noticed. By using this natural, nonaggressive approach, along with patience, endurance, and gentleness, you can shake the habitual power these "shitty" aspects have over you, and they will wither away on their own. It's like having stray cats roaming around your backyard. If you feed them, they stick around, but when you don't feed them anymore, they will disappear after a few foodless nights.

Now that you have a better understanding of karma, get planting, my fellow gardeners!

7
TWO ASPECTS OF MIND

*As we encounter mind's raw, unpro-
cessed conceptual activity, the teachings
encourage us to utilize our natural intelligence to look dispassionately at mind
and emotions and sort through our
confusion and ignorance; in this way we
uncover our innate wisdom and clarity.*

—DZIGAR KONGTRÜL

I HAVE BEEN BLESSED with two wonderful neph-
ews, Aiden and Brady. Right now, Brady is
almost one year old, and Aiden is about two and

a half. As the older brother, Aiden naturally tends to be the wilder one. He's always running around, jumping from one toy to the next. He'll bring you upstairs, then downstairs, then before long decides he wants to go back upstairs! Brady on the other hand, is just the quiet observer, silently sitting there, taking it all in.

Being around them quite often, I have noticed how analogous they are to the two aspects of the mind: the doer and the knower. The doer, also called the thinking mind, is the part of your mind that's always moving. Similar to little Aiden running around from one toy to the next, the doer creates story lines, judgments, worries, expectations, cravings, fears, desires, anticipations, and all the rest—in short, all the stuff that keeps you from being content with *this* moment. The doer's nature is dissatisfaction, thus it is forever seeking beyond the present conditions of your life and is only temporarily satisfied, at best, as it seeks after the next big thing.

The knower, on the other hand, also known as natural wisdom, is the silent witness of it all. The knower is like a mirror, reflecting a perfect image of whatever is placed in front of it. It doesn't judge or criticize what the doer is up to, or what it sees, but rather takes it all in with open arms. It's similar to empty space, which freely allows all things to arise and cease within it. Brady, being so young, doesn't have the mind yet to judge what he sees, so just like the knower, he gladly takes it all in, occasionally letting out a cute burst of laughter or an intense bout of tears. Unlike natural wisdom, Brady needs to be fed and changed. . . .

Although it may seem otherwise, I am not actually saying the knower is better than the doer; both are necessary to live and function in this world, but meditation practice is about resting in the knower to keep check of the doer. You don't want your thinking mind to be the master, but rather you must learn to be the master of your thinking mind. If you know the nature of the doer is dissatisfaction, you're not surprised when you find your mind complaining or getting lost in commentary about what's happening. That's what it does! You don't need to suppress these thoughts, nor do you need to believe in them or act them out. Remaining the knower, you can observe the mind without being harmed by it, much like Brady can watch Aiden from a good safe distance.

With meditation practice you not only train to quiet the thinking mind but learn to stay and be with your open awareness, allowing yourself to directly perceive reality clearly, rather than becoming stuck in your limited judgments, views, and beliefs. When you work with the practices mentioned in this book, your mind will expand, and you will have more clarity and peace within you. With time, you will be less likely to get caught in the sticky web of your mind.

NATURAL WISDOM

Let's further examine the concept of the knower, or natural wisdom. Every single person in the world is born with the two aspects of the mind mentioned above (yes, even you). Natural wisdom underlies your confusion, suffering, and neuroses. This wisdom is the ability to be aware or awake no matter what circumstances you find yourself in. Your natural wisdom is like a mirror that reflects everything and anything that is placed in front of it, without adding anything extra. It reflects clearly and equally all things looking into it.

Imagine your natural wisdom as a vast openness, much like the sky, and all the thoughts, emotions, sensations, sounds, and sights you experience like passing clouds. Never rejecting one cloud over another, the sky doesn't choose favorites but, rather, lets clouds come and go as they will. Sometimes there are huge storms filling up the entire sky with clouds, yet regardless of what comes into the sky, it always remains vast and open. This mirrors the concept of natural wisdom.

Continuously observe yourself with the "knowing" aspect of your mind and in time you will begin connecting with deeper and deeper glimpses of what I have been calling actual happiness. With practice, you will learn to settle down your thinking mind and learn to rest in your inner spaciousness, allowing you to see your life and yourself with focused clarity. Using your natural wisdom as your guide, you can step out of the way and let your life naturally unfold.

THE THREE FLAVORS OF EXPERIENCE

Here's how things typically go down: Open awareness experiences something—a sensation, sound, emotion, thought, taste, or smell—and that experience will have one of three "flavors": pleasant, unpleasant, neutral. Pleasant experiences are the ones that feel good—typically what your mind is constantly seeking and attempting to maintain. Enjoyable sounds, beautiful sights, and pleasurable sensations are all examples of this category. Unpleasant experiences, on the other hand, are painful and uncomfortable. These include feelings, sounds, sights, people, situations, and so on, that are all disagreeable. These are the experiences your mind tries to either prevent or avoid at all costs. Lastly, neutral experiences are those that are neither pleasant nor unpleasant. They don't excite you, yet they don't threaten you either, so your mind will most likely pay little to no attention to these, or even block them out completely.

Now, at this phase where open awareness is reflecting the present moment, there aren't any problems, just a raw, direct experience of reality. In the mind of a buddha, things would end there. For example, a moment of emotional discomfort could arise but then cease without leaving a "stain" in their mind. There would be no unnecessary suffering added, as this enlightened being would not get lost in habitual reactions but, rather, would be fully present and respond appropriately and without self-concern. But for the rest of us foolish practitioners, the cycle of unnecessary suffering is just beginning to brew. The direct experience is interpreted by the thinking mind, and a mental/emotional reaction immediately arises. Pleasant experiences create cravings and desires, which make you endlessly want more of the object in focus. Unpleasant experiences, on the other hand, birth hatred and aversion, causing you to lash out or run away from what you are perceiving. If mindfulness were strong, even this phase of the cycle wouldn't be an issue—a reaction arising is simply a reaction arising—but typically what happens next is your thinking mind grasps on to the reaction, believing it to be who you actually are. Immediately, your world shrinks to the fulfillment of desires or the acting out of aversion. A self is born, volitional actions follow, karma is created—and the end result is a lot of unnecessary suffering.

The practices of meditation and mindfulness taught in section 2 are so useful because they will allow you to open up to every experience—pleasant, unpleasant, or neutral—and help you see the cycle of suffering explained above clearly, so that you may have a chance to step out of it. Sure, it's easy to relax into pleasant conditions, anybody can do that, but as soon as things get rough or uncomfortable, there's tension and a desperate desire to escape. Learning to relax into any of these three flavors of experience, via connecting with your natural wisdom rather than identifying with the thinking mind, will help you stay with the direct experience of your life and connect you with a peace beyond this endless flux of flavorful conditions.

THOUGHTS: THE BURPS OF YOUR MIND

It's easy to believe your thinking mind's thoughts are a true interpretation of your self and your life. You are the only one who experiences your thoughts, so believing that the chatter in your mind defines who you are doesn't seem so strange. In reality, though, your thoughts are no different from, say, when your body burps. Certain causes and conditions create gas, which then exits the body in one of two ways. For argument's sake, let's stick with the burps. The gas leaves the stomach and is released through the mouth, only to dissipate into the space around you. I have never known anyone who has identified with the gas leaving his or her body. A burp is a burp, and it's not who you are, but rather something that just comes and goes on its own based on certain causes and conditions of your body. Your thoughts, on the other hand, are also created by causes and conditions (your personal karma) and come and go as they please, similar to burps. This is why I call thoughts the burps of the mind. They come up, make some noise, and then they disappear back into the silence from which they came. When you practice seeing the mind this way—as a natural release of thoughts rather than your personal identity to cling to—you may find that you can take your thoughts less seriously.

SECTION II

Applications & Practices

8
MINDFULNESS

Mindfulness is the aware, balanced acceptance of the present experience. It isn't more complicated than that. It is opening to or receiving the present moment, pleasant or unpleasant, just as it is, without either clinging to it or rejecting it.

—Sylvia Boorstein

So what's the first step you have to take in order to find actual happiness? It's awareness of this very moment. Remember, everything is happening right now. There is no other time. Freedom, peace, liberation, joy, suffering, sadness, birth, aging, sickness, and death are all found in this moment. In order to understand your life and yourself, you must first come to this understanding.

Imagine yourself trying to function in complete darkness in a house with no lights. You will always be stumbling around and bumping into things, since you can't see where anything is. Now imagine that you finally get hold of a candle and are able to light it. At first, the light is dim because the wick is fresh, but it's enough for you to at least see what's right in front of you. Now you are able to see things before you walk into them. As the flame grows larger you begin to see more and more of your house. You are able to find the shades that have been pulled down and open them up, flooding your house with so much light that you can finally find your way effortlessly through the entire space. This is exactly the situation that most of us find ourselves in. We are living in total darkness, unaware of this moment, unable to see the deeper aspects of our lives—and more importantly, of ourselves. Our minds are constantly dragging us back and forth between the past and the future, our likes and dislikes, our hopes and fears. Unfortunately, many of us dwell in this darkness because we are afraid of what we might find if we turn on the lights. On the other hand, some of us are unaware of the fact that the lights can be turned on at all.

The light in the analogy above is referring to mindfulness. Mindfulness is the ability you have to be aware, or awake, no matter what circumstances you find yourself in. It's the courage to be still and to let go into the flowing stream of life. Mindfulness is the tool that dispels all ignorance and lights up all darkness, cutting through delusions and illusions. With mindfulness you can undo ancient habits of the mind and learn to equally accept and welcome pain and pleasure, gain and loss, praise and blame, fame and humiliation, and so forth.

Training in mindfulness is not a difficult thing to do; it's as simple as paying attention to your next breath. All you need to do is be present moment after moment, without judgments or expectations, and without trying to chase after pleasure or run away from pain. The good news is you can be mindful everywhere you go, whether you are sitting, walking, eating, or even sitting on the toilet. With mindfulness training there is freedom—a spaciousness in your mind—that allows you to let go of thoughts and emotions, permitting them to pass through your awareness like a falling autumn leaf, effortlessly floating down from a high branch.

To further clarify, mindfulness can be understood as a nonjudgmental, intentional paying attention to the unfolding of your present-moment experience. It's very simple—but not necessarily easy! In fact, all too often you may find yourself doing quite the opposite of being mindful. This opposing state of mind, *mindlessness*, is very scattered; one in which there is little to no peace. Mindlessness happens when you *aren't* aware of what's going on in your mind. Much like the example above, you are literally functioning in the dark—completely unconscious of yourself and your behavior. The result is this: whatever enters your mind takes control of your words, actions, and speech, and instead of responding appropriately and spontaneously to the world around you, you instead react habitually and automatically to it.

Amid mindlessness, a rude comment or remark would immediately spark anger. Because mindfulness is not in control of the wheel, so to speak, the seat at the control center of your mind is empty and anger jumps right in, causing you to act or speak from it. Of course, this only escalates the situation and things keep getting worse as two unconscious angry egos continue digging into each other. Had you been mindful in that moment, you would've noticed the arising of anger, and through clear seeing of what was happening, would've been able to choose the most appropriate response to defuse the situation. This response wouldn't have been habitual or controlled by the anger itself but, rather, would've been the appropriate response for this specific situation. This is the power of mindfulness!

Mindfulness teaches you how to see your thoughts and emotions clearly, but more importantly, allows space for you to not identify with or limit yourself to either of them. Gradually, and with much practice, you can become fully grounded in mindfulness, giving you the freedom to use thoughts and emotions only when necessary, and allowing them to flow freely when they're not.

9
MEDITATION

Don't just do something, sit there.
—Sylvia Boorstein

ONE OF THE MOST ANCIENT and reliable ways to train in mindfulness is through the art of meditation. Meditation is typically done in a seated position (although there are many varieties, such as lying down or walking) and involves gently refocusing the mind on an object. A common object of meditation is your breath, more specifically the experience of breathing, and it is used as a way to stay in touch with the present moment without coloring it with your thoughts or judgments. Whenever your mind wanders away from your breath, be it a thought, daydream, or fantasy, you tell yourself that you're thinking, let the thought go, and gently bring your awareness back. By continually bringing your mind back to the present moment, you continuously stay awake and mindful, allowing sensations, thoughts, sounds, emotions, and whatever else you experience to freely come and go, without judgments or aversion.

I know it doesn't sound like much, but it's a profound training that teaches you how to be fully present with yourself and cultivates the ability to leave your thoughts alone. If you look carefully, you'll see that getting stuck in the passing thoughts of your mind produces much of your unnecessary suffering, and being able to let them go, even if it's only for one breath in seated meditation, will begin to set a new way of being in motion; a way that leads to freedom and actual happiness.

The practice of meditation is like owning a teashop with no door on it, welcoming everyone and anyone to stay as long as they would like. With respect and loving-kindness, you greet whoever arrives, invite them in, and serve them tea. Even scary, crazy people; even ones shouting at you or shaking their fists. All of them are allowed in.

During meditation practice you let your mind become like a mirror, perfectly reflecting and welcoming your experience without adding any extra judgments, comments, or beliefs. This will allow you to be very clear about what's happening. With practice, the concentration and mindfulness cultivated from meditating every day will spill out into your daily life. Instead of being tossed around throughout the day by your likes, dislikes, hopes, desires, and fears, you will be more open and trust in the unfolding of your experience.

There's a story from *The Book of Awakening* by Mark Nepo that depicts the message of mindfulness training. It's about a guru whose student was always complaining about the suffering in his life. The guru had him fetch some salt with a glass of water, pour the salt into the water, and drink it. The student was asked how it tasted, and he of course replied that it was bitter. The guru then brought the student to a lake and told him to mix the same amount of salt into the lake and drink from it. The guru asked how it tasted, and the student said it was fresh. The guru wisely explained that the suffering in life was pure salt, nothing more and nothing less, and that the amount of suffering he experienced depended upon the container in which he put it. He told his student to stop being a glass and instead become a lake. With the practice of meditation, you train yourself to become the lake so that the suffering in your life doesn't have a bitter taste.

Talking like this, it's easy to think that meditation is a magic pill you take in the morning and miraculously all your problems go away—but understand that problems will forever come and go and the pains of life are inevitable. There is no finish line, and there's never a time when you finally get it all together once and for all. On a positive note, with consistent practice you will find that there will be more clarity in your life and a calmness that will allow you to stop creating additional suffering for yourself. Over time, there will be a new relationship to the difficulties you face, and there will be more space in your mind to allow the thoughts and feelings that come along with such difficulties.

THE PURPOSE OF MEDITATION

When practicing meditation, it is very easy to get caught up in ideas of gain and loss. Meditation can feel all kinds of ways: sometimes peaceful, sometimes agitated, sometimes vast, sometimes narrow. Because there are many experiences that you can have while meditating, it's easy to feel like you have gained something when the experience is pleasurable or lost something when it is not. It's to imagine that one way of feeling is "good" and "right" and another is "bad" and "wrong." For example, one day you may feel full of bliss while sitting and think, "Oh yes, now I have finally got it," and other times you may experience anxiety, loneliness, or a deep sadness and believe that you must be doing something wrong.

I know this experience intimately. For many years I was caught in this cycle of gain and loss, and very recently, while on a meditation retreat, I was taught a simple way to remind myself of the purpose of meditation practice: the three Ss. The three Ss are reminders of the purpose of meditating and an easy way to align with its essence. They are:

Simplify.
Slow down.
See clearly.

Simplify is the first of the three Ss. With meditation you are simplifying both your body and your mind. Normally your mind is jumping all over the place, trying to run errands and make appointments throughout your day, but with meditation practice you are retraining your mind to simply be with each breath. By using the breath as an anchor in the present moment, while letting go of thoughts as they arise, you are simplifying the mind.

The second of the three Ss is *slow down*. Similar to simplify, slowing down is what actually occurs as you build your meditation practice. In the beginning your mind is like an untrained puppy running around, doing whatever it pleases. Your meditation training is like teaching that puppy to sit and stay. Over and over again you tell it to stay, yet all it wants to do is keep running away, but with time, patience, and perseverance, the puppy eventually learns to slow down and be still—at least for a little while. By focusing your attention on your breath and allowing yourself to relax, you are taking your wild mind and teaching it to just be right here.

The third *S* is *see clearly*. Through meditation practice you are able to experience your thoughts and emotions clearly, along with a variety of sounds and sensations. You know exactly what you are experiencing each time you sit, and more importantly, you are able to know things for what they are and learn to let them go. For instance, let's say you begin sitting and start to get anxious. With this anxiety come thoughts, story lines, and maybe even daydreams that keep the feeling alive, churning away in your body. With meditation you understand anxiety for what it truly is—simply an uncomfortable passing energy, manifesting in some specific ways in your body and mind: perhaps there's a tension in your chest, a rush in your ears, a thought that rises again and again, calling for your attention. None of this is a problem. They're just arisings.

Meditation helps you practice not becoming ensnared by the thoughts that come along with the feeling because you see how your thoughts arise spontaneously and vanish all on their own. You realize that your thoughts may not be accurately portraying the true situation of your life, or of yourself, but, rather, are just an interpretation, a story, layered on top of the sensations of anxiety; just a reaction to the sensations of anxiety. Being able to see all of this clearly allows you to let thoughts be thoughts, feelings be feelings, and sensations be sensations. By neither grasping them nor believing them to be who you are, you are able to let your thoughts and feelings go, let them be, and lastly, let them flow. Remember, in meditation you are cultivating the ability to leave things alone, and when you do so, you're left feeling more at ease with your body and mind. Eventually, these thoughts and feelings no longer linger as they once did.

The three Ss not only are a great reminder for the purpose of meditation practice but are also great to follow as guidelines in your daily life. Simplify yourself by remembering to be content. Truly, you need very little to be happy. Try to find happiness right here and now—with the things you already have. Slow down. Stop rushing to get through your day. The only place you're rushing to is the end of your life. Use mindfulness to take the time to feel each step as you walk and each breath as you breathe. Hear the sounds and see the sights around you, and truly enjoy the mystery that is your life. Finally, see clearly each and every unique moment of your existence.

No matter how repetitive things may seem, every moment is a once-in-a-lifetime experience. Be grateful and cherish the short amount of time you have on this beautiful Earth.

BENEFITS OF MEDITATION

There are many benefits to having a daily meditation practice. On a physical level, meditation reduces stress. Stress is known to create tremendous amounts of negative side effects on your body. It lowers your immune system, raises your blood pressure, screws up your digestion, and can even lead to heart disease. Stress keeps your body in the fight-or-flight mode, which is a very active, agitated state. All of this originally evolved in the brain of early humans as a means to survive out in the wilderness when confronted with wild animals or other dangers. Unfortunately, in the twenty-first century, it's true that you still *may* confront a wild animal or two, but it's more likely that the "wild animals" take the shape of figuring out how to pay your mortgage, dealing with your boss, sitting in traffic, and all the other wonderful irritations that get under your skin on a day-to-day basis. A mode that was originally intended for use in short bursts to ensure survival has now become the constant state of your body and mind, which leads to both mental and physical disease.

Meditation also benefits your emotional life. The process of labeling your thoughts as "thinking" and then letting them go without judgment creates what Buddhist meditation master Chögyam Trungpa calls "unlimited friendliness" toward yourself. Normally when thoughts arise, you grasp on to them and believe them to be true, and maybe even believe them to be the essence of who you are. These thoughts are loaded with judgments, such as good or bad and right or wrong, and come well equipped with a vast array of feelings that can sometimes pack a mean punch. In meditation, you train to let thoughts and feelings come and go, and with time you learn to untangle yourself from the story lines that have been keeping you a prisoner for so long.

On a grander scale, a steady meditation practice also benefits your life as a whole because you are clearer and calmer in your daily routine, allowing yourself to be less likely to make mindless mistakes. As your mindfulness increases, you will be clearer about your moods, thoughts, and reactions, responding to others with clarity rather than on a first impulse. You will also be able to read others better. Knowing when people are entangled in their emotions and closing down, you will learn how to better diffuse situations. You will also learn when it's appropriate to walk away and reschedule when things aren't working out in the moment.

When you become less stressed and more self-aware through meditation, your body and mind will be healthier. You will feel more comfortable in your own skin and become less caught in the story line of your thoughts, memories, hopes, anxieties, fears, and emotions. With ever-increasing clarity, patience, and perseverance, you will be able to prevent future suffering for both yourself and those around you. But keep in mind, this process is not about becoming a "better" you but, rather, understanding and accepting who you *already are*, while letting go of that which plants seeds for future suffering.

STARTING A MEDITATION PRACTICE

In order to start a meditation practice, you first need to know how to meditate—obviously.

To begin, you need to find a quiet space that is comfortable for you, away from distractions. You can use your basement, your bedroom, or even your closet if it's big enough. It's important that the room is tidy, as a messy room may agitate your mind. Make sure the ringer on your phone is shut off, and if you live with others, let them know what you are doing so they will know not to bother you. Set a timer for the allotted amount of time you'd like to meditate. Five to ten minutes in the beginning is enough, but eventually you'd like to get up to at least twenty minutes. Of course you are welcome to do thirty minutes, forty-five minutes, or as long as you'd like, but be kind to yourself and don't try to be a meditative super-hero right out of the box.

Once you have decided on a place, you can choose a seated position that works best for your body. You can sit cross-legged directly on the floor, or you can purchase a meditation cush-ion and sit on that. You may also want to try kneeling on a special meditation bench, or on a turned-edgewise meditation cushion if your body is not accustomed to sitting cross-legged. If none of those options are comfortable for you, then you can just simply sit in a chair. It's all good.

You'll next want to make sure you have proper posture. The way you position your body will affect the state of your mind. For example, if you slouch over or lean your back against a chair or wall, your mind will likely get hazy and you may fall asleep. This is not what meditation is about. You are not trying to zone out in some half-awake, half-asleep state, but, rather, you want to be fully aware and engaged with the present moment. In order to do this, you must have an upright posture. Sit with your back straight, let your hands rest palms down on your thighs (or fold them comfortably in your lap), and release your shoulders, dropping them away from your ears. Slightly tuck in your chin and gently close your eyes, or keep a relaxed, downward gaze a few feet in front of you.

Once you are positioned correctly, you can start your meditation by taking three deep breaths. Breathe in through your nose, breathing deeply into your belly (your belly should expand out with each deep breath in, just like an infant would breathe). Fill your lungs completely, then slowly release the breath out of your mouth, relaxing your body as you do so. After three breaths like this, breathe naturally in and out of your nose. Notice the state of your body and mind, without judgment. Continue to relax your body from head to toe.

Now bring your awareness back to the breath. Feel the sensations of the breath as it goes in and out of your nose. Keep your mind here. When a thought arises, whether pleasant or unpleasant, do not judge it. Rather, silently label it "thinking" and return to the sensations of the breath. As you sit, do not suppress any sounds or sensations you may experience. Let it all be in your awareness as you gently refocus your mind back to the breath. It's important to try to really remain still, even when an impulse to move or scratch or shift arises. See if you can notice the arising of those impulses without acting on them, and just return to your breath. Do this until your timer goes off, and then slowly begin to move your fingers and toes. Bring some movement into your body, and when you are ready, you can open your eyes fully. It is important to not just get up and rush out of meditation. Make the transition smooth. Move with mindfulness.

Try doing this meditation once or twice a day. The best times to do it are right when you wake up and again right before you go to bed, although any time you can make it work is fine. But it is nice to start and end your day with stillness and quiet, instead of the normal chaotic thinking and worrying. Dedicate yourself to this practice for a month and see how you feel. It may not be easy, but you can definitely do it. Just keep showing up and sitting each day. Eventually, you may even start to notice the space in your mind becoming vaster. If it helps, find a friend to do it with you, or join a local meditation community. Having others to sit with makes it much easier to be consistent.

COMMON MISPERCEPTIONS OF MEDITATION

Often people misunderstand the point of meditating. Many are under the impression that they need to *achieve* something, such as a special state of mind (I totally fell for this one when I first started), or that they need to somehow *stop thoughts* from arising in their minds. Others just don't feel as though they have the time to "waste" just sitting and doing nothing. These misperceptions lead to a disinterest in practicing meditation and cause most to just give up on it altogether.

It's not the case that thoughts need to be stopped when practicing meditation. As discussed earlier, your thoughts are not to be annihilated—they're just to be noticed and then released. Your mind was made to think, and although it may slow down and there may be moments of stillness, thoughts will always be arising and ceasing. Don't make such a fuss over them! Without thoughts we wouldn't be able to function in a society. The idea that thoughts must be stopped not only is the wrong approach to meditation but also fills your head with the impression that your thoughts are bad, creating an internal war between the object of meditation and your thoughts. This leaves you tenser than you were before you began. Warring with yourself is the complete opposite of what you are trying to do when you sit and meditate.

Let go of the struggle. There need not be any wars in your mind during your practice. Label your thoughts "thinking" and then let them go, even if it happens a thousand times in your session. They are not keeping you from peace, nor are they distractions, just simply your mind moving—no big deal. With time, thoughts become nothing more than a bird passing through an open sky, leaving no trace (well, except maybe for the shit on your shoulder—but that's what laundry detergent is for!)

Another common misperception is that there is some great mystical experience to attain. Although peak experiences may transpire during meditation, this is not the purpose of your practice. Peak experiences, like all things, are impermanent and don't last. It is easy to want more experiences once you've had one, especially when they feel good. If they are held on to or yearned for, they can actually block you from deeply experiencing the present moment, which is really the whole point of meditative practice. Remember, all you are doing is simplifying, slowing down, and seeing clearly; you are learning to stay with all of yourself without judgment, practicing being present, and cultivating your natural wisdom.

Folks often say something like, "I just don't have the time to sit and do nothing." This actually has two wrong ideas about meditation combined into one. The first is that you need a lot of time to practice. The funny thing about people is that they make excuses when they do not see the value in things. They don't have five minutes to meditate, but if their car broke down or their child were sick, there would somehow be time to fit it all in—it's all a matter of priorities, isn't it? As mentioned before, you only need to take five to ten minutes a day to start your practice. If there is no time in your day to do this, wake up a little bit earlier, or go to bed a few minutes later. If that is not an option, go sit on the toilet at work once a day for five minutes and breathe. I'm quite sure no one will bother you there! The bottom line is, whatever you have to do, do it, because a little bit of effort over a long period of time goes a long way.

The other part of this misperception is the false belief that you are sitting there doing nothing while meditating. These days, we like to fill up our time *doing* things. We have become "human doings" rather than human beings. We are, as the poet T.S. Eliot once said, "distracted from distraction by distraction" and never have time to be still—to be present. Sitting in meditation is far from doing nothing. When you sit, you are fully engaged with your life and fully in touch with yourself. You are not running away or escaping from your problems; you are facing yourself without distraction and without the masks of daily life. There is nothing in meditation but you and your direct experience of the moment. By practicing, you are coming to thoroughly understand and know yourself. Through understanding and knowing yourself, you will learn to love and accept yourself, and by loving and accepting yourself, you will learn to let go of yourself. When you are able to let go of yourself, you will have found the freedom and peace that has been there all along—actual happiness.

10
JUST SAY YES

The first step toward change is accep-
tance. Once you accept yourself, you open
the door to change. That's all you have to
do. Change is not something you do. It's
something you allow.

—WILL GARCIA

IN CHAPTER 8, I mentioned the first step to begin living your life deeply and peacefully is to bring yourself here into the present moment. The next step is to say *yes* to what's here. Right now, in this very moment, fully accept whatever you're feeling—whatever is happening in your life, whether you are in pain or experiencing pleasure, whether you feel on top of the world or you're at your low-est of lows. Just for a moment, see what it's like to stop pointing fingers at your parents, to stop wor-rying about losing more weight, to stop thinking about the coworker you can't stand, to stop hoping for more money. If those things arise, just allow them to be, without getting sucked in. Let go of the story line of your life with all its thoughts, memories, hopes, and fears, and just experience the freshness of this moment. Feel the sensations in your body. Hear the sounds around you. Stop reading. Seriously. Put down this book and just be completely present with yourself for three full breaths.

How did that feel? Were you relieved? Did you become more anxious? Was your mind con-stantly spewing out thoughts? Whatever you experienced actually was perfect. Again, and I can't say this enough, there is no certain way you're supposed to feel. You only need to relax and open up to what's there, and the wonderful news is that "what's there" is always new and fresh. Everything is always in a state of movement. So if you felt great, awesome! That will change. If you felt crappy, awesome! That will also change. If you didn't feel anything . . . well, you get the point.

Remember, peace cannot happen in some future fantasy, such as when you finally hit it big and win the lottery, find that perfect partner, rid yourself of negative emotions, or become enlightened. All of these ideas are future projections and found only in your mind, not in reality. Reality is right here in this very moment where you may not have enough money, or where you may be lonely without a partner, or where you may have plenty of unpleasant emotions that you'd rather not deal with. When you are present with your actual situation, rather than some ideal fantasy, you will come to see that things are workable and there is always space in your mind. You are never stuck. Only by being present and clear about what's happening in this moment can something be done, but the very first step is to just say yes.

Paradoxically, at the same time that you are saying yes, you must also be willing to say no—and this is where the idea of renunciation comes in. Ordinarily, renunciation is understood as getting rid of something; historically, religious clergy of all faiths have renounced things such as drugs, alcohol, and sex (some have even renounced talking) in order to deepen their commitment to their faith. Unlike these monks, priests, nuns, and so on, who traditionally renounce material things or desires, the renunciation I am referring to has to do with getting rid of your own *resistance* to how things are right now. It's as if you are bowing to each experience with a certain respect and surrender. I'm reminded of the famed author and Buddhist teacher Jack Kornfield's quote that captures the essence of renunciation best: "To bow to the fact of our life's sorrows and betrayals is to accept them; and from this deep gesture we discover that all life is workable. As we learn to bow we discover that the heart holds more freedom and compassion than we can imagine." Instead of closing down or shutting things out, this kind of renunciation allows you to have a more liberated way of being in the world. I want you to open fully to the whole experience of your life. Renounce all struggles and just be with what is: the sufficiency of the shitty, foolish self that's here, and all the details of that shitty, foolish self's life. Through practicing renunciation in this way, you will be able to accept things just the way they are and say yes to every experience.

A common misperception of saying yes is that you just accept everything and never take any action: if people are walking all over you, you just accept it; if you lost your job and cannot afford food for your family, you just accept it; if you're rude to everyone you meet, you just accept it. This is not the purpose of saying yes. It's true; saying yes is about fully accepting this moment. Being your shitty, foolish self is, of course, all about accepting yourself and your life just as it is. But this isn't the end of the story.

Think of it in this way: instead of just passively accepting life as it passes you by, think of this practice of saying yes as a kind of *dynamic acceptance*. This dynamic acceptance is the ability to be fully present without resistance, so much so that you can be completely engaged with the present moment from a place of clarity and deep acceptance. The acceptance part is only an internal letting go of the struggle between what you *wish* your life to be and what's actually present. It allows you to be clear and honest with your current situation but in such a way that you can respond from a place of clear seeing rather than habituation. Only after saying yes, without all the stress of "this shouldn't be happening," can the true work begin. Whatever is present in your life is here, and that's just the fact. Gently lay down the struggle; accept it and work dynamically from that place of acceptance.

11
SHENPA

"Shenpa" is the urge, the hook, that triggers our habitual tendency to close down. We get hooked in that moment of tightening when we reach for relief. To get unhooked we begin by recognizing that moment of unease and learn to relax in that moment.

—PEMA CHÖDRÖN

NORMALLY when you hear the word *addiction*, you may think of extremes such as alcohol or drug abuse, but the truth is, you too are an addict. What is it that you are addicted to? Well, to put it quite simply—yourself! You're addicted to your own point of view—to all of the beliefs about yourself, others, and the world around you—and lost in the judgments, opinions, emotions, and story lines that constantly run through your mind. The truth of the matter is you are the only thing getting in the way of actual happiness in your life. The good news is you don't have to try so hard to change anything about yourself to reconnect with it—you only need to take yourself a little less seriously.

There are many ways in which you can take yourself less seriously, but one of the most beneficial teachings I have found for this is that on *shenpa*. *Shenpa* is a Tibetan Buddhist term that was first introduced to me by Pema Chödrön in her audiobook *Getting Unstuck*. Her instructions on working with shenpa have definitely been the most useful and transformative teachings I have encountered thus far. Shenpa is typically defined as "attachment," but Chödrön explains that it's more of a "stickiness," or a "hooked" quality, although that still doesn't quite capture its true essence. My favorite description is her analogy of shenpa as poison ivy. Chödrön clarifies that shenpa can be likened to the rash one gets from poison ivy. This also includes the itch of that rash and the burning desire to scratch that itch. The rash itself would be your thoughts and emotions, all of which are charged with their own unique "itch" that, when present in your body and mind, creates the desire for you to "scratch." The itch she is speaking of is a certain response to whatever arises.

For example, if you are driving and some-one cuts you off, anger arises (the early stage of shenpa). Not only will anger arise, but thoughts and urges to act upon the anger will also arise (the itch). Finally, you open your window and stick up your middle finger, waving it around at the inconsiderate driver who had the audacity to cut you off (the scratch). Similar to a rash spread-ing from scratching at it, following these desires to act makes it easier for similar reactions to arise again and again and again. By continually react-ing in the same way, you create habits or karmic tendencies that become deeply engrained in your mind, feeding your own personal miniaddic-tions. These repeated reactions and actions lock you into a self-created prison and make you feel unable to escape the narrow world that you your-self built.

Shenpa is a common quality found in every single human being in the world—including you—and unfortunately any feeling, whether bad or good, can be the starting point for the desire to "itch" and "scratch." As you start bringing mindfulness into your life, you will notice which thoughts and feelings—good or bad—hook you the most. These will be the ones that you can't seem to let go of or put down very easily; they usually have the most emotional charge. By working with these emotional charges rather than acting on or hiding from them, you will learn to diffuse their power at an early stage and not let them grow out of control. With patience and perseverance the shenpa in your life will decrease. As I have been repeatedly saying, you don't need to try so hard to change yourself; you only need to stop letting the stickiness of your thoughts and emotions run the show.

Working with your shenpa is actually quite simple, but as you'll learn very quickly, simple doesn't necessarily mean easy. In order to work with shenpa, all you need to do is notice when you have been set off—and not act on the habitual response. It sounds simple enough. When the driver from the example above cuts you off, the first thing that happens is an immediate tightening sensation in your stomach. This tightening is like you striking a match, and if you are not careful, that little flame can spread in no time, engulfing all that comes in its path. If you are able to notice yourself being pulled into the flame, so to speak, you can stop and tend to the feeling instead. Try to stay with the actual sensations in your body while observing the thoughts that come and go along with it. Try to let the thoughts go, for they are like gasoline and will only continue to feed and spread the flame. Find where you feel this rage, or any other difficult emotion, inside you. Where exactly do you feel it? What does it feel like?

Continue to let go of the thoughts and story lines and connect directly with the sensations of the body instead. This way you are stopping the momentum dead in its tracks, and the habitual chain reaction will not occur as usual. If you are able to just stay with the emotion, it will eventually go away on its own—remember: everything that arises, ceases—and you will have taken a step in the direction of less future suffering for yourself and those you encounter. Keep in mind, emotions are not a problem; they are only passing energy moving through your body. Learn to ride them out by letting go of the thoughts until they decide to leave.

A while ago I had a career change and started a new job at a private school for children with autism. I found a similarity between how I was taught to treat disruptive behavior with one of the children there and my personal practice of working with my shenpa. Instead of using aggression or punishment in response to the child's disruptive behavior of swatting at my face, I was taught to gently hold his arms down to protect myself, and calmly sit, waiting until the struggle ceased before attempting to regain instructional control. I wasn't punishing the behavior, nor was I giving him the sense that it was wrong or bad. I wasn't rewarding the behavior either; rather, I was showing the child that this behavior would not get him anywhere. No reactions or attention, be it positive or negative, would be gained from acting out in this way.

Similarly, when I experience difficult emotions, I calmly sit and wait out the emotion. I neither suppress it nor act on it but, rather, become a mirror, perfectly reflecting the energy as it passes through me. The emotion is now able to do its little dance and leave without causing harm to me or those around me. Of course, it is not always as simple as it sounds.

EXTINCTION BURST

Your reactions to the world around you have been habituated over years of chasing pleasure and escaping pain. Growing up, you most likely wanted to feel good and fit in. You wanted to be loved. These yearnings for love and acceptance are natural, and because of them your mind has created ways of being in the world, or better put, habits that have kept you safe and secure growing up in an imperfect and groundless world.

Whether you had an abusive parent, experienced a major trauma, or even simply had an older sibling who you thought was "better" than you, your environment has molded your behavior. In fact, there's a good chance that you identify deeply with the ways you've *learned* to be. Reacting over and over again in the same way to the people, places, and things in your life has become a very strong habit. Sometimes these ways of being become outdated and outgrown, yet the habitual power, or shenpa, they carry is still so strong that they become a burden in your life; and as with any habit or addiction, an extinction burst should most definitely be expected. An *extinction burst* is a term used in the psychological field of applied behavioral analysis and literally means a burst of activity that occurs when a habituated behavior is in the process of extinction.

To clarify, every behavior has a reward, and when the reward is no longer available, the natural response, before the behavior becomes extinct, is to try harder and harder to get it. Imagine a lab rat that has received a pellet of food every time it pressed a lever in its cage. If no food was given one day when the rat hit the lever, the rat wouldn't just press it once and give up; rather, it would keep pressing the button over and over again in hope of obtaining the pellet of food. This burst of the behavior is an example of an extinction burst. If the rat were never fed again via the lever, it would eventually learn to not even bother pressing it, but not without a few last frantic attempts to get its reward.

So why the hell am I talking about extinction bursts, lab rats, and food pellets? You may be wondering what this all has to do with shenpa. Well, as you work with yourself, you may find old habits and behaviors falling away, and with the letting go of these, you may experience many difficult emotions, such as fear, grief, or deep existential anxiety. Being mindful of your thoughts and emotions and how you relate to them may become overwhelming at first. You may feel like these practices are making you worse at times—more thoughts, more emotions, and more intensity. The reality is you are just becoming aware of what has already been there, and on top of this, extinction bursts may make it seem as though you are falling apart or going stark raving mad.

Let's say you reach for a drink every time you become anxious, and you begin noticing this as you practice mindfulness and meditation. You start seeing how harmful this behavior is becoming and how strong your shenpa is for having yet another drink. The numbing sensation that temporarily rids you of all your problems is something you crave, especially when you are feeling anxious about your life. Noticing the pattern of your cravings, you decide to try working with the shenpa, and instead of immediately reaching for a drink when you feel the tightening of anxiety in your stomach, you decide to try and sit with it instead. Neither suppressing nor acting on the craving, you practice feeling the feelings and learning the story lines that accompany them, and you try to breathe through it until it passes. The first bunch of times you attempt to do this, you may find that it will seem impossible. As you're sitting with the craving, it keeps growing and growing until it becomes so strong that you finally say "screw it" and go down a Jack and Coke. The growing intensity as you decide to not follow these cravings *is* the extinction burst itself. Your body and mind crave the reward, and they're going to kick and scream until they get what they want, unless of course you wait long enough for them to give up. Luckily, impermanence is on your side.

We're not necessarily all alcoholics, drug addicts, or sexaholics, but there are many subtle habits and behaviors that make up who we think we are that can be just as hard to release. For instance, you may have a habit of being quick to snap around your parents, trapped in a negative pattern of lashing out. If this is the case, then feeling the tension and allowing some space when you are in their presence may be difficult at first, especially with the extinction burst that will come when you begin trying to let it go. With practice, though, you will eventually be able to go beyond the intensity of the extinction burst, and with time, things may begin getting easier and easier. You will not perfect this skill, and many times you will just watch yourself do the harmful behavior, but don't get down because of this. Be patient with yourself, and be kind.

This is part of the ongoing, lifelong process of working with shenpa.

ATTACHMENT AND AVERSION

The teachings on shenpa are so beneficial because they point to the fact that your thoughts and emotions, in and of themselves, are not the real issue. What a relief! The problem lies only in your attachment or aversion to them. The more you attach to something, the more you suffer. On the other hand, the more you run away or try to avoid something, the more you will also suffer. Let's investigate this.

When it comes to attachment or aversion, you are generally caught in what Buddhists call the eight worldly concerns. According to the Buddhist tradition, the eight worldly concerns are a major source of your suffering. They are grouped into four pairs of opposites:

- The hope for happiness and the fear of suffering
- The hope for fame and the fear of insignificance
- The hope for praise and the fear of blame
- The hope for gain and the fear of loss

Happiness, fame, praise, and gain are typically associated with attachment because these positive experiences can bring you pleasurable sensations and thoughts. With both of these comes an intense craving for these sensations to last longer or become more intense. As previously mentioned, all of us want to be happy and no one wants to experience suffering. Living this way may have been a useful characteristic for our ancestors' survival, but it has actually now become a main reason for why we suffer. Because of this underlying desire of always wanting to be happy while avoiding suffering, we desperately try to hold on to pleasant experiences. We just love that damn warm puppy! Not only do we try to grasp on to and continue these pleasant experiences, but we also constantly crave more of them. This method to happiness will only increase your suffering. Remember, if your happiness is based on worldly possessions, emotions, or states of mind, you will never be able to pin it down, since all of those things are constantly flowing and changing. It's like trying to pin down a butterfly with the hope that you will somehow forever catch its beauty. After a few days of its being pinned up on your wall, you'll find that your beautiful butterfly will turn out to be only a rotting, dead bug. Once things don't go according to your plan, or once the good feelings start to fade or change, you will see the suffering of your attachment.

On the other hand, suffering—feelings of insignificance, blame, and loss—produces instant negative sensations and thoughts, which, when faced, create a determination to evade, escape, or reject the experience. Have you ever heard that whatever you try to get rid of you will get more of? Well, in a really important way, it's true. If you try to get rid of all the suffering in your life, it will only cause you more suffering. As discussed earlier, some suffering is inevitable and can be avoided for only so long, but your aversion to suffering only makes it worse.

It's clear that both paths—hope and fear—lead to only one place: suffering. If you take a good look into your emotional life, you will most likely find yourself to be lost in one of these eight worldly concerns. So what are you supposed to do to become free of them? Work directly with your attachment and aversion. First, realize that you are caught up in one of them. Know that you believe the story lines you tell yourself. See how tightly you are holding on to your interpretations of how things should be. Then try to accept that you are getting stuck and, as taught in the shenpa teachings, feel the feelings, learn the story lines, and watch them as they do their dance. Recognize the suffering of holding on to the attachment or aversion to what's happening, and breathe through it. Most importantly, don't take yourself so seriously. If you are unable to let the story lines go, no big deal! Instead of getting down on yourself, simply try to observe what it's like being caught in the attachment or aversion. What does it actually feel like to be stuck? Is there suffering? What would letting go look like in this moment? By paying attention to your stuckness, you will give rise to wisdom and compassion. You see? Even messing up can be enlightening, and I promise you, life will give you plenty of opportunities to practice working with both attachment and aversion. So you'll get many chances to master it!

ODYSSEUS HAD THE RIGHT IDEA

In her book *Taking the Leap: Freeing Ourselves from Old Habits and Fears*, Pema Chödrön refers to Homer's *Odyssey* for another great example of working with your shenpa. In this Greek epic, the hero Odysseus is obliged to cross a perilous sea in which dangerous temptresses, called Sirens, are known to lure men to their deaths through the sweet sound of their voices. Odysseus had been warned about these Sirens, so he ordered his seamen to put wax in their ears in order to drown out their beautiful songs. Odysseus, on the other hand, decided he wanted to hear the Sirens, so he ordered his men to tie him to the mast of the ship and instructed them not to untie him, no matter what he told them. As they passed the island of the Sirens, Odysseus was able to hear the voices but was unable to act on and follow their tempting seduction, saving his own life and those of his men.

Now, for all of you ancient-literature buffs out there, this may not be the most accurate retelling of the story; my high school English teacher was not the most engaging instructor and my maturity level was not up to par, but I think you get the point. You, young grasshopper, are Odysseus, and the Sirens are your thoughts, emotions, desires . . . your shenpa. So you have three choices: suppress, follow, or mindfully be aware, neither suppressing nor following. You can choose to be the men with wax in their ears, completely ignoring the beautiful, alluring sounds; the previous sailors whose boats crashed on the rocks; or Odysseus, securing yourself to the mast of meditation and mindfulness. Clearly option three is the most desirable, as you will be able to hear the beautiful tempting sounds of your desires, attachments, and fears without becoming ensnared by them.

12
THE TWO WINGS
OF MEDITATION
PRACTICE

Know emptiness, be compassionate.

—MILAREPA

THROUGH THE PRACTICES of mindfulness and
meditation, you will begin to notice how every
single problem always has to do with you. Whether
someone said something that offended you, or you
find yourself at a job you hate, whatever it is—it's
all about you. "When will I be happy?" "Why can't I
ever find the right lover?" "Why don't I feel the way
I want to feel?" "Why is this happening to me?"
Notice a pattern? *I, I, I. Me, me, me.* Think about it.

When has a problem *not* involved self-concern? Never! That's when. So what's the conclusion? Stop thinking about yourself all the time!

Now, when I say stop thinking about yourself all the time, I am obviously not saying *never* think of yourself. In fact, the previous chapters discussing meditation and mindfulness are all about you and discovering the wisdom and peace you already possess. But wisdom and peace are only half the story.

On a retreat once, Simon Child, one of my teachers and a dharma heir of Chan Master Sheng Yen, gave a talk about the two wings of meditation practice. The first was wisdom, and as mentioned earlier, wisdom comes from deeply observing yourself in each moment of your life, realizing more and more the insubstantial nature of self. The second wing was compassion, and just as a bird with only one wing cannot fly, your meditation practice will not be able to take off until you have both wisdom and compassion flapping away. Only with the practice and cultivation of wisdom *and* compassion are you able to chip away at your addiction to yourself. In the next chapter, we'll explore some of the practices that can help you cultivate the compassion side of things.

13
COMPASSION

If you want others to be happy, practice compassion. If you want to be happy, practice compassion.

—Dalai Lama

A WHILE AGO, while visiting my mom, I learned that our neighbor's grandson had passed away. I was in shock, not only for his loss but also because I did not know he even had a grandson. I soon found out that he had an older son whom I had never met, who lived in Pennsylvania. He was now in town for his son's cremation. As I went over to share my condolences with the family, I ran into my neighbor and his grieving son just as they were about to pull away in their car. I told them how sorry I was and asked if there was anything that I could do for them. My neighbor's son introduced himself as Jim, thanked me for stopping by, and jokingly said as the two drove off, "I could use a case of beer." When I returned to my house, I saw that my mother had already bought a card for the family. I offered to bring the card over with, of course, a six-pack of beer. I dropped it off with my neighbor's wife and continued on with my day. About an hour later I was packing some things into my car when Jim came outside to greet me. He came up to me with a big smile and eyes of gratitude and said, "I was only joking, but thank you." We hugged and each went on our way.

Although I had never met Jim before that day, this brief encounter made me feel as if I had known him all my life. The care and concern I felt for him were equal to what I would expect to feel for those closest to me. His suffering was my suffering, and all I wanted to do was alleviate his pain, even if it was only by getting him to crack a smile with my six-pack delivery.

Like an apple tree whose only purpose is to produce and freely give away apples, without expecting anything in return, your purpose, too, can be focused on giving your time and attention to alleviating the suffering of all beings. This is commonly known on the spiritual path as *compassion*, and it is a main teaching of most religions. Without compassion your meditation practice can become too self-centered and incomplete. When you start bringing mindful awareness to your life, you begin to understand that we are all in this boat together. You find we are in a world where things fall apart and are constantly in a state of change. You learn that aging, sickness, and death are the only guarantees in life, and because of this we *all* experience pain and suffering. No one escapes this truth. Although frightening at times, you can bravely use this knowledge to go beyond the differences you have with others, allowing yourself to see your shared humanity and your shared suffering. Seeing the pain of others as your own is a step in the direction of cultivating compassion, and there has never been a more important time than now for you to do so. Look around today and find the Jims present in your life.

Place your self-concern aside, and put your compassion into action—even if it's only in a small or simple way.

CULTIVATING COMPASSION

Although there are many ways to cultivate compassion, I have found that they can be approached from two directions: compassion for yourself and compassion for others.

While these may seem like complete opposites, you will come to see that the two are actually inseparable. The more compassion you cultivate for yourself, the more you will have for others, and vice versa. Essentially, the compassion you have for yourself should be equal to that you have for others, but unfortunately this is usually not the case. I mainly meet people who have great compassion for others but barely any for themselves.

Through my experience I have noticed that many people can listen to the problems of their friends and family, and no matter how messed up those problems may be, they withhold judgment and feel compassion; yet as soon as the tables turn and the problems are their own, the judgments and self-hatred come rushing in. Why is this? Why do we care for others so much and so little for ourselves?

Personally, I am very familiar with this. As a mindful-living trainer, I tend to hear about the difficulties, failures, and shortcomings of my clients, and have no problem listening with a big heart and warm, loving attention. But for many years, I was unable to direct that same kindness toward myself. When I would "mess up," by lashing out in a heated moment of anger or falling into some unwholesome habitual patterns, I would hold myself in contempt. I believed that as a spiritual practitioner I should "know better," and would be deeply disappointed with myself for not being *holy* enough. For a majority of my spiritual path, I had otherworldly standards, ones that were impossible to actually keep up with, and when I didn't live up to them, I would drown myself in shame and disappointment. Turns out, all of this idealism was actually fear of my emotions and not having practical tools to help me relate to them appropriately. It was a kind of "spiritual act" I could put on to show the world I had it all together, when underneath, the truth was actually quite the opposite.

I now see myself with much kinder eyes and understand that I don't need to become a spiritual superhero simply because I meditate and have a spiritual path; nor do I have to become anything special or show off how "holy" I am. Rather, I can allow myself to be ordinary, nothing special, and continue on my journey of reducing suffering in my life and those around me to the best of my ability. I will say this though; I am much better off than I was when I first began this path, and I've definitely released trying to live some unattainable ideal life of perfection. And do you want to know something? I can now confidently say, "that's just fine with me." My practice now seems to be this: rejoicing when I am able to respond out of wisdom rather than neurosis, but also rejoicing in the fact that sometimes I am unable to do so. When this happens, instead of berating myself, I've learned to practice cultivating compassion and loving-kindness. I use the understanding of how difficult it is to work with my own struggles, even with all the tools and knowledge of mindfulness and meditation I have, and connect with those in a similar situation—some of whom don't even know these practices even exist!

It comes down to this: we need to face the simple fact that we are human and we are going to make mistakes—often, actually. With the wisdom you uncover from practicing the meditation and mindfulness techniques in this book, you will learn to see clearly the choices you and those around you are making. This can sometimes be very painful, but rather than feeling bad about these choices, you can celebrate the fact that you are aware of them and can allow yourself some compassion. Making mistakes unconsciously and in complete ignorance is very different from making them in full awareness with compassion. Rather than reprimanding yourself about your mistakes, look back and reflect on where things went wrong. You may not always be able to stop yourself from repeating them, but you can be very clear about how you were triggered and how you could have better handled the situation. After this short reflection, make a commitment to do it better next time, and then simply try again next time. With awareness and compassion you will learn how to feel the heartbreak of negative actions without falling into self-hatred or denigration, and instead increase your dedication to freeing yourself from them.

So how do you cultivate compassion? There are many ways in which you can do so, but let me share two of my favorite methods: *metta* and *tonglen*.

Metta means "loving-kindness," and metta meditation was one of the first techniques for compassion that I learned. I remember it like it was yesterday. I was on my very first three-day meditation retreat. It was a beautiful Saturday afternoon at the retreat center when the teacher introduced the group to this powerful method. Here is what he taught us: First, start off in a comfortable seated position, keeping your body relaxed yet upright. Come into the present moment by taking a few conscious breaths. Next, bring to mind someone whom you love dearly— someone who brings up that warm feeling of loving-kindness within you. It could be someone already passed or still alive; it can even be one of your favorite pets. Sit with this feeling until your entire body is filled with loving-kindness. The first phase of this meditation is to wish this loving-kindness toward yourself. You can do this by silently repeating these four phrases as you sit in meditation:

> May I be safe.
> May I be happy.

May I be healthy.
May I have a peaceful mind.

These are only an example of what you can wish for yourself. You can always change these phrases into whatever fits best for you and your unique situation, as long as it is said with the intention of well-being for yourself. For example, if you are struggling with an addiction, you could try repeating these phrases: *May I be free from the struggle of craving. May I find peace in my heart. May I be content.* Or maybe you are someone who has much self-hatred for your body, and your practice could sound something like this: *May I learn to love myself just as I am. May I find happiness in who I already am. May I learn to love myself unconditionally.* The best way to pick the phrases for yourself, is to allow a response to arise effortlessly. Bring your struggles into your mind and see what comes out of the depths of your heart.

It's important to understand that this practice of metta is not about making yourself feel a certain way, nor is it about ridding yourself of hurt feelings or other uncomfortable emotions. Instead, it's about cultivating a warm, loving space that can open you up to a deeper level of compassion. For example, you may notice during your first time trying this practice some major resistance to wishing yourself loving-kindness. Rather than using the phrases to push out this resistance, allow them to gently redirect the mind to the path of loving-kindness. Feel the resistance. Notice where it's felt in the body and what thoughts are associated with it. Why is it so hard for you to wish loving-kindness to yourself? Explore this! Then let the thoughts go and return to your phrases, giving the resistance space to be there while you do so. At some point, your heart may crack wide open and you may actually feel deeply loving-kindness toward yourself.

The second phase of this meditation is to think of someone close to you, such as a good friend or a family member. You can picture them in your mind, smiling and full of joy, and start directing the loving-kindness toward them. In this phase you can just replace the *I* with *you* (e.g., "May you be safe"). When I do this phase, I will actually say the person's name before the phrase (e.g., "John Doe, may you be safe"). There are no strict rules as to how you do it; it's really all about the intention behind the wishing.

The third phase is a little harder than the first two. In this phase you try to think of a neutral person in your life. This would be someone you see, whether once in your life or every day, but have no real relationship with. A few examples of a neutral person would be a bus driver, a cashier at your local grocery store, or even a random person walking down the street. In this phase you are learning to cultivate loving-kindness for the people who normally mean nothing to you. In doing so, you are making every person in your life real—people just like you who want to be happy and free from suffering. Seeing neutral people in this way is the beginning of cultivating compassion for all beings.

The fourth phase is by far the most difficult and takes a lot of courage, effort, and patience to work with. In this phase you are wishing the same loving-kindness that you had for yourself and your close friends and family for someone toward whom you have negative feelings, traditionally called one's "enemies." You follow the same method as before, but this time you fill in your enemy's name. You may *want* to say something like, "John, may you stop being such a jerk," but try to keep it similar to the examples above.

Sounds pretty crazy, right? It *is* pretty crazy and goes against the grain of normal thinking, but let me tell you, it can truly transform your heart and mind. I've used this many times with people who have upset me, and it really helps cool the flames of anger. I don't necessarily love the people who cause me trouble, but this practice keeps me from limiting myself to my own unwholesome thoughts about them. The constant effort of wishing them loving-kindness transforms the future encounters I have with them and allows me to see past their unwholesome actions to the fragile human being behind those actions. Metta practice doesn't mean I have to *like* the difficult people in my life, nor must I go out of my way to try to be their best friend, but it helps remind me that they are doing the best they can with the wisdom they have at this moment in time. Just like me, they get continually stuck in certain ways of thinking, speaking, and behaving, but also just like me, they have the capability to wake up and do something about it. Practicing metta leaves space in my mind for me to see this potential within them.

The final phase of the metta meditation is to include all the people from the previous phases and equally send them loving-kindness. You can imagine them all in one room together, smiling and full of joy, as you repeat the four phrases. In this phase you can say something like, "May you all be safe . . . happy . . . healthy . . . with a peaceful mind." If you're feeling extra generous with your loving-kindness in this phase, you can wish it to all sentient beings. Imagine every single being in the world receiving your message of compassion and love.

Although these five phases can be done in one sitting, there is no rule as to how you do it. You may not be ready to wish loving-kindness to your enemies or to those you don't know, and you know what? That is totally fine! See which phases resonate with you and your life at this time, and work with that. I've heard that Jack Kornfield has been known to tell his students to do one full year of loving-kindness meditations just for themselves. Take an honest look at what you need right now, and work with that.

The metta meditation is not only for seated meditation. It can also be used on the spot in any situation. For example, if you see a homeless man on the street, you can wish him health, happiness, and so on. Or maybe a family member is suffering through a disease or illness. During your visit you can repeat the phrases silently to bring out the loving-kindness in yourself for them. Although your wishes may not necessarily cure that person, the good intentions will keep you in the state of mind to love this person in whatever way you can at this time. Just try it out and see how it goes.

The second method of meditation is called *tonglen*. This method is a little more radical than the loving-kindness meditation, but it's a great way to transform suffering of any kind into compassion; it also lessens self-concern. Tonglen, typically translated as "sending and receiving" or "giving and taking," is a Tibetan Buddhist meditation practice in which you visualize yourself taking the suffering of others while also sending them joy, peace, and happiness. Similar to the metta practice, tonglen can be done both in seated meditation and on the spot. It can be broken down into two parts: working with your own suffering and working with the suffering of others.

Let's start first by working with your own suffering. Any suffering you experience can be used as a way to cultivate compassion for yourself and all beings. If you are home sick, feeling crappy with a cold, you can breathe in the suffering you are experiencing and fully accept the uncomfort-ableness of it. As you breathe in, you can connect completely with your suffering while holding the intention to free others from similar suffering. Now here's the radical part: as you inhale, you are not only wishing for others to be free from their suffering but actually imagining yourself removing and voluntarily *receiving* their suffer-ing, voluntarily taking it on. Another way of say-ing it is that you are visualizing experiencing your suffering *on behalf* of others suffering that way. This process is typically done by visualizing the suffering of others as black, heavy smoke and inhaling it through your nose into your body. By practicing in this way, you are lessening your self-absorption and reversing the ancient mindset of avoiding pain and discomfort. When you exhale, you can send health, peace, and joy to all of those people who are feeling just like you. This positive, healing energy can be visualized as a white light emanating from your body to all other beings.

The practice of tonglen can be used to give any suffering you experience meaning or pur-pose. Instead of the normal response of turning away from a painful situation, you are coura-geously facing and accepting it with the intent to remove that same suffering from others. With each breath you are also equally feeling and accepting both your suffering and the freedom from that suffering. Although it's obvious that you will not miraculously heal the entire world of their cold symptoms or any other forms of suffering, you will be cultivating a compassionate mindset, which can also lessen your own self-concern and the fear of pain and discomfort.

Tonglen can also be done when you experience the suffering of others. If you know someone who is suffering from a disease or illness, you can breathe in their suffering with the intent of taking it from them, while breathing out health and happiness. If breathing in their sickness is too intense for you, then you can just breathe in with the intention that they will become free of their suffering. Although breathing in the suffering of others may seem frightening, I recommend trying it when you're ready as it is a tremendously profound and transformative practice.

Similar to the metta meditation, tonglen can also be done on the spot. If you see someone driving angrily in traffic, you could breathe in their anger and send them the peace of mind you may be capable of. Or if you see a hungry person on the street, you could breathe in the hunger and send out satiation and nutrition (and of course you can also buy the person food, give them a dollar, or donate to a relevant charity—on top of doing tonglen). It's great to use tonglen on the spot for any form of suffering, discomfort, or pain, because rather than turning away from what you are seeing, you are facing it head-on. When you first begin to practice tonglen on the spot, you may feel the need to verbalize your intent: "Angry driver, may I take your anger, freeing you from it, and give you my peace of mind." As you become more proficient, your intention may become more simplified, breathing in anger and breathing out peace. However practiced, know that you are training to become fearless and, ultimately, compassionate.

You can also use tonglen when you experience pleasant situations, or feelings. It doesn't always have to be about suffering! Anything that brings you joy or happiness can be sent out into the world. If you wake up feeling great about life, send out that good feeling with the wish that all beings could feel this way when they wake up today. Did a loved one surprise you with a thoughtful gift?

Send out the feeling of being loved to everyone you know—and even those you don't!

Try this: Whether things are going your way, or the complete opposite, use whatever today brings you as a way to practice sending and receiving. Share any pleasures and joys by sending it to all beings. If you encounter suffering, breath in that suffering—taking it from everyone feeling the exact same way—and send out relief.

14
FORGIVENESS

An eye for an eye will only make the whole world blind.

—Gandhi

A FEW MONTHS AGO a friend confided to me about a tragic end to his most recent relationship. After weeks of suspicion and the feeling that something wasn't right, he found out that his girlfriend of two years was cheating on him. When he confronted her, she was full of denial. Unable to deal with both the selfishness and the dishonesty, he took his things and, completely heartbroken, walked out of her life. About a month later he received a text message from her in which she apologized for cheating and for the pain she had caused him to go through. She asked him to meet up so they could speak to each other. Although his pain was still fresh, he decided to see her and talk it out. As they spoke, his heart opened when he saw how much pain she was in for the mistake she had made. Seeing her vulnerability and how sorry she truly was, he was able to forgive her more easily and move on peacefully with his life, grudge-free. Eventually they were able to become close friends and, as far as I know, are still in touch with each other.

Situations such as this happen all the time, and although not all of them have this particular ending, their example clearly shows how forgiveness is not necessarily for the person who caused you harm but, rather, for yourself. Forgiving someone allows you to release the burden of anger, hatred, and rage that would simmer inside you if you decided to hold tightly to a grudge. Of course, forgiveness can also be healing for the person who harmed you, but *your* peace of mind is equally important.

Now, you may not believe in forgiveness, so let's consider the alternative option: holding a grudge. If you hold a grudge against someone who has harmed, embarrassed, or hurt you, every time you see or hear about them you will feel enraged, with all kinds of uncomfortable emotions stirring inside you. While you are at home feeling sick to your stomach, the person who harmed you could very well be sitting on a beach in Hawaii, happily sipping on a mai tai. To whom is the grudge really bringing harm? Does this person even care that you are angry with them? Probably not! Clearly the only one who suffers from holding a grudge is you, so what is the point of doing that? It seems logical, rather, to forgive and release the burden so you can move on peacefully with your life. Here's a traditional analogy that clearly demonstrates what I am talking about: When you carry a grudge, it's like holding a burning hot coal, waiting to throw it at a person who has brought you harm. Sure, you *might* be able to bring some pain to this person by flinging a hot coal at them—but they can just duck! And in the meantime—immediately—you will be burning your own hand.

While this concept of forgiveness sounds all fine and dandy, the reality of practicing forgiveness is that it's not always going to be easy. Forgiveness cannot be forced and shouldn't be faked; rather, forgiveness is going to be a journey of opening up, expressing, and releasing your hurt feelings. Contrary to what some believe, the practice of forgiving takes strength and lots of courage, and it is definitely not for the weak-hearted. More importantly, forgiving someone needs compassion as its support. Being able to see the person's humanness or vulnerability may make it easier to forgive, and this can be done through the compassion practices found earlier in this book. We all make mistakes. We all get confused sometimes. We all hurt others with our actions and words at times. We should all be able to be forgiven and have chances to start over and try again.

As you embark on this path of mindfulness, remember to also be kind to yourself. Forgiving yourself for your mistakes is crucial to a peaceful mind and healthy body. These mistakes include harmful thoughts, words, and actions directed toward others and especially toward yourself. When you accept your shitty, foolish self, you put aside your self-hatred and make room for compassion. When you practice self-forgiveness, you no longer hold yourself in contempt, which is infinitely better than being weighed down by guilt, unable to deal with the next situation that arises. In other words, being so caught up in what you did wrong yesterday leaves no room for the things you can do right today.

How does one actually achieve forgiveness? Is it as simple as saying, "I'm sorry"? I don't think so. As you could have guessed, there is a practical approach to working toward forgiveness. When you think about it, there are really only three situations where forgiveness might be needed: hurting yourself, hurting others, and when others hurt you. In each of these instances someone's been hurt, and there is a need for forgiveness.

So, how can you start doing this? If you'd like to begin practicing forgiveness, here's how you can proceed. First, get yourself into a comfortable and upright-seated position, as previously described in this book. Bring yourself into the moment with a few deep breaths, then close your eyes and recall a situation that you feel requires forgiveness. Be open and accepting of all the feelings that arise within you during this time, and depending on the situation, gently repeat a phrase of forgiveness for yourself or for the other person. Although you may find it difficult at first, what's important is that you're allowing yourself the time and space to embrace the hurt and set the intention of forgiveness. After all, the mere fact that you're sitting down and thinking about it is more than most people would do. Many are more likely to set aside a time in their busy lives to watch *American Idol* or *The Bachelor* than practice self-awareness. Imagine if everyone sat down, even just for five minutes a day, to practice a little forgiveness. We would live in such a nicer world.

When I practice this form of meditation, I generally sit for twenty minutes, but any amount of time you can dedicate in your daily or weekly schedule should be sufficient. The freedom derived from this act of meditation is not likely to happen in one sitting—especially if the situation was intense—so continuous effort is recommended. (Please note, in the case of serious and overwhelming circumstances, this method may not always be enough. If the pain you are experiencing is beyond what you can handle, you may want to seek the appropriate professional attention.) You may find with continued practice that you are slowly becoming more able to forgive. Forgiveness is about letting go—allowing the pain to heal so that you might achieve the peace of mind you really desire.

Maybe you don't have to pick up that hot coal quite as often. Release it from your hand and be done with it.

SECTION III

Putting It All Together

15
INSPIRATION
The Key to Peace

*The secret of discipline is motivation.
When a man is sufficiently motivated,
discipline will take care of itself.*
　　　　　　　—SIR ALEXANDER PATERSON

IT'S IMPORTANT to find ways to stay inspired in order to maintain a steady meditation practice. Without inspiration your practice will slowly diminish and eventually be nothing at all. Personally, I have found my inspiration through reading books. In the past several years, I have read and reread hundreds of books on meditation and mindfulness. I learn something new from each book I read and am also reminded of why I am doing all of these practices to begin with. For me, reading is a way I can keep a fresh perspective on living mindfully.

If books are not your thing, there are plenty of other options out there for you. Start simply. Take a walk on the beach or in the woods and surround yourself with the beauty of nature. Spend time with children and learn from their simplicity. Make yourself more childlike rather than child-ish. Once you begin to feel more comfortable with the practice, you may even want to go on retreats, watch talks on YouTube given by respected medi-tation teachers, or listen to audiobooks as you are driving in your car. You might want to seek sup-port in Buddhist communities, where other med-itators are trying to make peace with their own shitty, foolish selves. Whatever works for you, just do it! Find the people, places, and things that keep you inspired to practice, and do your best to surround yourself with these motivational forces. Inspiration is a positive, motivational energy—a flowing stream that leads to an ocean of peace.

16
GOING DEEPER

When a man knows the solitude of silence, and feels the joy of quietness, he is then free from fear and he feels the joy of the dharma.

—THE BUDDHA

MOST OF THE PRACTICES in this book have been directed toward your everyday life, and although it's essential to use each moment of your life as your path to awakening, it is equally important to take some time away from all the distractions of daily life. It's possible to do this on your own, let's say in a cabin deep in the woods, but I have found that being in an organized retreat setting run by experienced meditation teachers is best. Many of my personal retreat experiences have been at one place, Dharma Drum Retreat Center, in the tradition of Chan Buddhism, founded by Master Sheng Yen. On retreats you are able to sit with the rawness of your experience without the distractions of social interactions, cell phones, and the normal busyness of life. You are able to investigate your mind: how it runs away from the present moment, how it creates its own suffering, and so on.

I was even lucky enough to do a work-study program, where I lived and practiced at the retreat center for a full month. Although there are hundreds of places to practice meditation retreats, I have found Dharma Drum to be the best fit for me personally. If you choose to go on a retreat, you should do your homework first—research and find the best center for you in your area. Maybe try out several. Many different faith traditions offer retreats, so find the one that is most comfortable for you and your beliefs, but keep in mind that Buddhist retreats are mainly centered around the practice of meditation. So if you'd like to go deeper into your own meditation practice, it may be wise to sit with a Buddhist community on retreat, as it will be the core focus of the time spent there. Remember, you don't need to convert to Buddhism to go on a Buddhist-style retreat and to reap the benefits of a weekend in silence.

You may be wondering, "What exactly is a retreat?" In the Buddhist tradition, a retreat is a period of time that can be one to three days, all the way up to weeks, months, and even years, where mindfulness and meditation practices are strictly followed. During a retreat, there is usually a strict schedule of sitting meditation, walking meditation, and even work practice that is followed throughout the day. At most retreats all of these activities are done in complete silence. Being silent is an important part of being on retreat. Silence means that you neither talk to other people nor engage in meaningless chatter to yourself in your own head. In this way, you are able to directly experience each moment, breath, emotion, and event throughout the entire day, without the distractions of other people or your own thoughts. Silence on retreat also means that you don't have to look around at other people; there's no need to smile at someone, look gratefully at someone who held the door for you, and so on.

Although these gestures may not literally be *saying* anything at all, they can set off a ton of thoughts in your mind and distract you from your practice. For example, imagine an attractive person (of whatever variety you prefer) happens to be on retreat with you, and at some point you accidentally lock eyes with them and they send you a quick smile. Instead of having a nice, relaxing retreat where you can focus on the methods of practice, your mind will be filled with fantasies of how you are going to run off into the sunset together and live this wonderful life of love and passion—all of this over a silly little smile (when in reality they were probably thinking, "Why is this creep staring at me?").

Not only are you silent, but you are also asked to move slower than the normal hustle and bustle you are used to; there is no rush to get anywhere, and the activities are coordinated with the sound of bells, singing bowls, and wooden blocks, all of which are explained at the beginning of the retreat. There is no need to worry about time, food, or where to go next, as this is all taken care of by retreat coordinators and volunteers.

Most importantly, all electronic devices are shut off and stored away. There is no reading, writing, emailing, calling, or texting. All you have is your own body and mind. You may not find all retreats to be exactly this way (many may not even be silent), but this has been my experience at Dharma Drum, and I have found this environment, schedule, and etiquette the best fit for my meditation practice.

To help give you a better understanding of what happens on a retreat, let me share a sample day I have experienced. Depending on the intensity of the retreat, a typical day will start around four or five in the morning with an obnoxiously loud banging from the morning boards—a hammer hitting a plank of wood. Trust me when I tell you that you will not need an alarm! There are three rounds of the morning boards that will give you three chances to try to get yourself out of bed at the crack of dawn. After you empty your bladder, brush your teeth, and wash your face, you're off to the meditation hall for some morning exercises. The morning exercises are gentle stretches and moves that encourage mindfulness of the body and loosen you up for the full day of meditation to come.

Following the morning exercises is the first period of meditation (often about thirty to forty-five minutes per sitting), followed by a morning service—a shortened traditional Chan service in which everyone can chant a variety of sutras, vows, offerings, and so on. This is especially nice, as it allows you to use your voice during long days of no talking! After the morning service it's time for breakfast. . . .

Breakfast, like all activities during retreat, is in complete silence. If you're anything like me, when you eat on any other normal day outside of a retreat setting, you're either thinking of a million other things or driving to your next appointment; you're definitely not focused on the experience of eating. On retreat, though, eating is another form of meditation. You are able to take the time to taste the food and feel each bite as you chew. Over and over again you bring your mind back to the experience of eating. It's definitely a strange yet liberating experience. Once breakfast is over, you then have your first round of work practice. On the first day of retreat each person is assigned a simple task to keep the retreat center clean and tidy. I tend to always get bathroom duty or dishwashing—my two least favorite things to do.

The idea behind this, yet again, is mindfulness—keeping your mind focused on the task at hand and gently bringing it back when it wanders off to thoughts of all the fun and loud activities that you could be doing instead of silently cleaning toilets on retreat.

When you finish with your task, you then have some free time to rest before a Dharma talk, a talk given by the teacher of the retreat on the practices and struggles you may encounter—and an entire morning of sitting and walking meditation. Then there's lunch, and another work practice. The afternoon is filled with more bouts of seated and walking meditation until evening service and, finally, dinner. Once dinner is completed, there is one last rest period before another Dharma talk, followed by more periods of sitting meditation. Around nine-thirty you get to go back to your room for "lights out" at ten.

My retreat experiences have been amazing, and what's so wonderful about them is that each one is unique. You will always learn something new about yourself. I specifically remember one retreat that was very transformative and healing for me. It was a five-day Western Zen retreat that used a Chan meditation method called the *huatou*. A huatou is a short phrase or question that is repeated and used as a contemplative object of meditation, as a way to take you beyond words to an experience of your true nature—your natural wisdom. On this particular retreat my huatou was "Who am I?" Over and over again I would gently ask myself this question and would acknowledge and release all the answers my mind produced. I remember the teacher of this retreat explaining that using this method is like cleaning out a garbage can with a mirror at the bottom; all the beliefs you identify with are considered the trash, and eventually you will get to the bottom and see your reflection in the mirror. Once you get through the first couple of layers of the mind, you eventually get to deeper parts.

A few days in, during a Dharma talk, I specifically remember the teacher telling us to search in places that we would never expect to look for the answer. I don't know what it was about what he said, but it pointed me to a deep-seated belief that I was alone. I had never felt that I was alone, but after hearing these words, the thought "I am so alone" popped up, and with it came a flowing of tears and sadness. After this my mind slowed down and eventually ran out of answers to the question. All that was left after my huatou was a still and quiet space. During an interview with the teacher, which is offered a few times on retreat for questions and advice, he said to me, "So, Mark, tell me who you are." There was nothing but peace and stillness, and I was able to respond simply, "This is who I am." Although this may not seem like a big deal, there was a profound difference between who I thought I was at the beginning of this retreat and who I really was at the end. After exhausting all the ideas about who I thought I was, all I was left with was a peaceful stillness— my natural wisdom.

Upon leaving retreats, I have always come home feeling refreshed and inspired. Going on a retreat is like recharging your mindfulness battery, allowing you to go back to your daily life with a deep inner peace and a motivation to continue your practice at home. As you go deeper, you may find this inner peace more easily accessible. This is the purpose of this book: to go deep within your shitty, foolish self to find that you are not limited by who you think you are. You are so much more than you can possibly think of, and retreat practice will definitely help you realize this further. As your mind quiets down and the layers of thoughts and beliefs fall away, all that's left is what has been there all along: the perfect person . . . you!

17
DON'T DRINK THE KOOL-AID!

To think that you will be happy by becoming something else is delusion. Becoming something else just exchanges one form of suffering for another form of suffering. But when you are content with who you are now, junior or senior, married or single, rich or poor, then you are free of suffering.

—AJAHN BRAHM

NOW THAT YOU have all of these new tools to work with, be careful not to fall into the trap of drinking the Kool-Aid! Drinking the Kool-Aid refers to becoming an imaginary, perfected version of yourself; it's a forced attempt to be "holy," so to speak. It's easy to notice when someone is drinking the Kool-Aid, as this person never faces the negativity in their life. Everything is love, happiness, rainbows, and unicorns. They overemphasize becoming a perfected spiritual being. Other signs of drinking the Kool-Aid are constantly speaking in an overly kind and gentle voice, eyes wide open with a fixed, creepy smile. The Stepford wives come to mind.

As a former Kool-Aid drinker myself, I shaved my head and attempted to emulate the holiness of Christ and Buddha. I engaged in outrageous acts of kindness on my college campus and preached the benefits of a meditative lifestyle to all and sundry (rather than just to people who at least expressed a little interest by buying my book). Overall, in that Kool-Aid phase, I just wasn't being authentic and honest. This fantasy was not long-lived, as I could not sustain this persona for very long. I am sure you have seen people like this before; you may have even seen me creepily roaming around Montclair State University in New Jersey, chanting mantras while fingering my rosary beads.

So what about this book? The practices found in this book are not meant for you to become someone else—they're meant to make you more yourself. From personal experience, I can tell you that when you are trying so hard to be a perfected being, you don't think very highly of yourself. You are definitely not accepting your shitty, foolish self but, rather, running away from the realities of who you are.

A good teacher can help you avoid the Kool-Aid—a problematic teacher might pour you a big heaping glass. Just as you would seek out a good doctor or therapist, use whatever methods you can to find a reputable teacher with whom you will be comfortable. A worthy teacher will not relieve you of your responsibility. You own your responsibility, and anyone who tries to take that away from you is trying to slip you a frosty glass of Kool-Aid. Be wary of a teacher who wants you to believe and follow with no questions asked. Also think twice (at least!) before handing over your life savings. Pay attention to the behavior of other followers. Do they look and dress the same? Do they seem as though they have no mind of their own? Do they practice rituals that elevate the teacher to a godlike status? If so, don't be a sheep;

run from those creeps! You should never feel pressured to act in a certain way or believe in anything a teacher tells you. I realize that you may be in a vulnerable state—I certainly was at the start of my own journey—but you must choose wisely, as there are many so-called spiritual leaders who are looking to take advantage of you and claim to have all the answers.

A qualified teacher is simply an experienced guide—someone who has trod the path you are now walking on—who provides a direction for *you* to walk at your *own* pace. Your journey belongs to you; therefore, only you have the power to accept your life and work with it. Throw out whatever teachings you don't connect with, and keep and incorporate into your life those that resonate for you. You can put your confidence in a teacher who will provide support and instruction as you do this work, but don't expect this teacher to hand you the answers and solutions to all of your questions and problems on a silver platter.

Accept the responsibility to do the difficult work of waking up. Only you can liberate yourself from your suffering, and you don't need to wear a phony smile or dress yourself up in a new spiritual wardrobe while you're doing it! Also, keep in mind that a good teacher will give you the tools you need, but ultimately you are the one who must build the house.

Stay true to yourself and steer clear of those Kool-Aid pitchers.

18
YOUR FEELINGS MATTER

If you don't look after your feelings, who will do it for you?

—THICH NHAT HANH

ALTHOUGH MOST OF THIS BOOK has been about accepting and letting go of conditioned reactivity and habitual story lines, it's very important to understand that your feelings do, in fact, matter.

You'd be drinking the Kool-Aid if you decided to disappear forever in the woods, determined never to become involved with any of your feelings or thoughts. That's cutting out a really important part of your essential humanity—and that's not what any of this is about. In order to function in the world we live in, you need to forge a relationship with your feelings and thoughts. The purpose of the practices found in this book is not to make you "nothing" but, rather, to give you the freedom to be fully yourself. For example, if someone is constantly abusing or taking advantage of you, don't just accept it and let it go. Your feelings matter! Stand up for yourself. Learn to communicate your feelings, say what you need—and walk away when necessary.

Sometimes the path of living mindfully and peacefully can be used as a way to keep you a prisoner of feeling unworthy. Just because you might be practicing a more accepting and open way of living and thinking doesn't mean you have to become somebody's doormat. Even the great spiritual teachers in history (e.g., Buddha, Jesus Christ, Gandhi, etc.) were committed to their teachings and beliefs and didn't back down in the face of their adversaries. It may seem logical to think, "My feelings have been hurt, but instead of making a fuss over it, I'm just going to feel the feelings and let them go like my meditation teacher taught me." But in reality, the underlying truth of this may be, "My feelings are not important, and I'm too afraid to stick up for myself." This thinking is fear based and not the way taught in this book. Correctly practicing meditation and mindfulness will help you become aware of your thoughts and emotions in a way that allows you to work *with* them, rather than allowing them to work *on* you. Remember, dynamic acceptance, not passive acceptance!

I recently had a conversation with a friend about how feelings matter. He was feeling a bit empty and was deciding whether or not he should stay in his relationship. These feelings were familiar, though, as they had been part of past relationships that didn't work out. He asked me if he should tell his significant other how he felt. I responded, "Of course! Your feelings matter. It's important to talk about them instead of acting like they shouldn't be there."

Just because your mind is saying *get out* doesn't mean that's really what you want. Talk to your partner, express these feelings, and see what happens. This is the way you get close to someone—by sharing your fears, hopes, and more importantly, your feelings! However messed up or *wrong* they may seem, find the courage to express yourself just as you are.

Again: at the end of the day, your feelings matter, and as important as it is to learn to let them go in order to not become ensnared by them, you must never think they are unimportant or unworthy of being expressed. A solid, healthy relationship with your own emotions and thoughts is the goal. I want you to be your shitty, foolish self, not "nothing" at all. Learn to see the flowing nature of emotions, but feel comfortable enough to use and express them in a way that still allows them to do their unique dance. Find ways to communicate your emotions without becoming ensnared by them.

19
YOU ARE NOT ALONE

You are never alone or helpless.
The force that guides the stars guides
you too.

—Shrii Shrii Anandamurti

IN YOUR DAILY LIFE you probably come across many people, all of whom when asked, "How are you doing today?" answer with a smile, "Great, thanks." But there is a great possibility that things are not as they seem. I know for a fact that when I answer this way, I am not always being honest. The truth is we show people only what we are willing to expose. Every day we put on the masks of who we want to portray ourselves to be, yet underneath these masks lies the truth that no one has it all together. Each one of us has our confusion, and we are all a little neurotic in our own unique ways. Sometimes our uncomfortable attributes make us feel very isolated, insecure, and alone. You may think, "If anyone knew how messed up I am, they would disown me or want nothing to do with me." This is not necessarily the case. I'm here to tell you that you are not alone. No matter how crazy you think you are, I can guarantee you that there are a whole big bunch of others experiencing the same issues as you.

You are not alone with your problems, and the only way you can experience the truth of this is by finding people open and honest enough to share their personal struggles with you. Last month I brought a friend to a Narcotics Anonymous meeting, as he had been struggling with a drug addiction. I knew he had been feeling down about his problem, so I suggested he go to one of these meetings to see that there are many others just like him, and lots who have been able to stay clean. Although it was frightening at first, he was eventually able to open up to the group and also hear how others had been dealing with the same painful addiction he was going through. Now he wasn't alone; he had a support system of like-minded people who could help him get through his drug issue.

Even if you are not an addict, you can still join groups, organizations, or communities that are geared toward mindful living. In Buddhism, a community of meditation practitioners is called a *sangha*. A sangha can gather anyplace, and the goal is to practice meditation together in a communal setting. Here, they share their stories, inspirations, and struggles. A sangha neither has to be run in any special way nor attended by thousands of people, although that has been known to happen. I have been a part of many sanghas—some that I created—that had only five to eight active members. I have found that being part of a sangha is crucial to my becoming both comfortable and accepting of my life. It's quite liberating to freely express your feelings and thoughts, without the worry of being judged or told your feelings are wrong. When part of a community, you may find that others are feeling exactly the way you do, and with the realization that you are not alone, you can face your problems knowing you are supported.

If you think you might be interested in joining such a group, it's easy to find one by simply
searching online or making a few phone calls. Be
sure to find a community that fits you best, and
don't be afraid to shop around a little; you want
to be comfortable with the members you will be
spending time with. If joining a random group is
not your thing, then be inspiring and start your
own. Grab some friends, teach them to meditate,
and talk about life. Have no expectations, and
see where it leads you. After a while you might
find it helpful to make arrangements for a guest
speaker, or perhaps your group might choose to
read an inspirational book together. There are
no rules, so feel free to change it up every once
in a while. Vary your environment; go on a "field
trip" to different places. You are limited only by
your lack of creativity and resources. The sky's
the limit!

20
LIFE AS A PATH TO AWAKENING

The path is the goal.
—GANDHI

WHAT'S SO WONDERFUL about the practices of mindfulness and meditation is that each moment of your life can be used as a way to wake up and not fall deeper into the sleep of ignorance. Growing up, my spirituality was limited to one hour each week—church—and the rest of the time was just ordinary life. This gap between the sacred and the mundane created a void that left me feeling spiritually malnourished. I think it's important to contemplate this point: If your spiritual practice doesn't include the entirety of human experience, why even bother doing it? How can you have a complete life practice if things are left out?

With the perspectives in this book, every thought, emotion, sensation, and situation can be used as a way to cultivate acceptance, understanding, and meaning. Even the worst times of your life can allow you to connect with all beings. After all, others also experience their own versions of what you experience. Anxiety is anxiety. Anger is anger. Love is love. Although the story lines may vary, the feelings are something we equally share. Any good feelings can be shared, spreading the peace and joy all around, and even the bad feelings can be used as a way to cultivate compassion for others experiencing the same thing.

I cherish the wisdom of the Buddhist tradition so much because there isn't a single aspect of your life it leaves out of the practice. Whether you are stuck in traffic when driving to work, rocking your child to sleep on a cool summer night, caught in a moment of anger in a heated argument with a friend, or sitting at the bedside of a dying family member—all of it is part of your path and can be used to point you in the direction of actual happiness.

Not only can your life be used as a path to awakening, but many Buddhist teachings also remind us that *our very lives must become the practice itself.* It's one thing to meditate once a day for twenty minutes, but it's another to live with the attention and warmth of meditation all the time. Actually, I make sure to remind my yoga students often of this. At the end of every class I teach, I explain the importance of bringing their practice home, and how the real practice begins when they roll up their mat and walk out the studio doors.

In fact, one of the very first teachings the Buddha offered, called the eightfold path, includes an entire section dedicated to practice off the meditation cushion. The eightfold path lays out a path from ignorance to awakening and is broken down into three sections: wisdom, concentration, and morality. The wisdom section includes right understanding and right thinking, which, in a nutshell, points to aligning with the Buddha's teaching of the four noble truths (or "things as they are") and directing the mind to thoughts of renunciation, loving-kindness, and nonviolence. This section lays out a conceptual road map of the truths of existence, and through investigation and deep contemplation, you slowly begin aligning yourself with what you find—literally making your experience itself the path of your practice. The concentration aspect of the path, which includes right effort, right mindfulness, and right concentration, deals exclusively with methods of meditation and mindfulness, which allow for deeper and deeper experiential understanding of these truths. Lastly, the morality section specifically points to how to live an ethical, awakened life, AKA the how-to guide for practice off the cushion. The latter section can be broken down further into right speech, right action, and right livelihood. Together, wisdom, concentration, and morality make an all-inclusive practical guide to living a meditative lifestyle, giving you all the tools you need to cultivate wisdom and compassion with every moment of your life.

Let's explore the three subcategories of morality further, as they seem to go right to the core of practicing with every moment of your life.

Right speech points to practicing with the words that come out of your mouth. As explored earlier, everything you say plants seeds that will bear fruit at some point in the future, so it's always important to choose your words wisely. In meditation, it's obviously easy to have right speech because you aren't talking to anyone—but pay attention to your silent inward speech as well. In daily life, on the other hand, words are almost always being exchanged with others. When you choose to have your life become your path to awakening, the way you speak to others becomes a very important, and oftentimes difficult, practice.

Knowing that your speech has a tremendous effect on your life and the lives of those around you, it would be very wise to pay close attention to what's going on in your mind during verbal exchanges. This ability to see clearly during a conversation is cultivated by the concentration aspect of the eightfold path, mainly through dedicating yourself to the meditation and mindfulness practices found in this book. Also, by keeping in mind right understanding and right thinking, you can begin trying your best to have your words in line with loving-kindness and nonviolence, speaking only what's true and timely. Just think about how much unnecessary suffering could be avoided if you simply refrained from telling lies, gossiping, and using rude, harmful speech. As easy as it sounds, I have to say I've often found it to be very difficult. Don't get me wrong, right speech is great and definitely the smarter choice, but wrong speech is juicy and quite seductive! It's very easy to get sucked into a gossipy conversation, especially if the person being talked about is someone you are not a fan of. But truth be told, actual happiness will *not* be a possibility if you are not practicing right speech.

Obviously, a big part of right speech includes how you are talking to others, but it also includes how well you listen to them too. When you are speaking with someone, are you actually hearing what they are saying? Or is your mind immediately filled with what you want to say back? Are you noticing the body language this person is giving off? Are you responding appropriately, or simply reacting blindly? Next time someone is speaking to you, listen to them without an agenda. This is a wonderful practice and is very helpful when working on right speech. As they speak, be completely attentive and available. Notice the tone of their voice and the way they are holding themselves. What are they *really* trying to tell you? Is their body telling you something different? Stay with them fully and you may be surprised how well you respond.

Right action, the next subcategory, aims at ethical, peaceful, and honorable conduct in everyday life. Oftentimes, it's taught as five precepts, which all point toward moral ways in which an enlightened being responds and lives their life. These precepts are as follows: not killing, not stealing, not misusing the body, not lying, and not intoxicating the mind. Although they may seem like the familiar commandments of Moses, they are not laws you must follow that are set in stone but, rather, guides for you to live by—ways for your life to be the practice itself. Much like all teachings in the Buddhist tradition, they are meant to promote curiosity and cultivation. They are pretty straightforward, actually. But much like right speech, practicing right action is much harder than you think.

A good way to use these precepts is to investigate and learn from the times you are breaking one of them, or at least thinking about it. For example, if you catch yourself lying to someone, become curious and ask yourself what you're trying to hide. Why did you decide to break this precept and not be truthful? If you find you keep waking up next to a new person every single weekend, pay attention and dig deeper. Look at what's really happening and learn from it. Is this way of life making you any happier, or is it only leading to more suffering? Be honest with yourself. Notice that none of these teachings are telling you to beat yourself up for breaking a precept, but, rather, they are having you honestly observe and reflect on how you practice your life, moment to moment.

Another way to use these precepts is to come at them from the positive side. If all of these "not"s are giving you heartburn, try to cultivate their opposites. For example, instead of practicing not killing, why not attempt to protect all living beings? Or rather than working with not stealing, try cultivating generosity through the practice of giving freely. It's probably best to practice the precepts from both the positive and the negative sides, but pick the one that fits for you right now. More importantly, use them to make every action your meditation practice.

Right livelihood is the last subcategory of morality and has to do with how you make your living. According to this practice, you must try abstaining from having a profession that causes harm to other beings or the environment. One example of an unjust livelihood is creating weapons intended to bring harm to others. This clearly goes against the precept of not killing and would not be the best choice for making a living. Using the precepts of right action can help you make a choice for a livelihood that would be blameless and honorable, giving you the peace of mind that comes from living innocently.

By using your life as a path to awakening, nothing is left out, and every moment is meaningful. In fact, as you've seen from the eightfold path, everything you do can be the practice itself. Whether it be speaking, acting, or the livelihood you choose, it can all be used to as a way to wake up and point you in the direction of actual happiness. More importantly, once you've chosen to use your life as a path of awakening, you will come to realize that being your shitty, foolish self isn't so bad after all.

21
FEARLESSNESS

People may use tranquilizers or yoga to suppress their fear. They just try to float through life. We have all sorts of gimmicks and gadgets that we use in the hope that we might experience fearlessness simply by taking our minds off of our fear.

—CHÖGYAM TRUNGPA

WHEN YOU THINK of someone who is fearless, you may think of a person who never experiences fear—a superhuman who can walk into any threatening situation, unfazed by the dangers that present themselves. The truth is that becoming fearless doesn't mean that you ignore fear or that it never arises. Fearless people absolutely experience fear, but the difference is they have become so familiar with it that it no longer cripples their actions. With the perspectives in this book you will begin to look honestly at yourself, your actions, and your reactions. Practicing meditation will help you learn more and more about how your mind works and how you can better deal with it when things get rough.

For all living organisms on the planet, fear is a primal emotion. Even a hermit crab shrinks back into its shell when it feels threatened, and you are no different in that sense. Fear is, without a doubt, a survival mechanism, a way to keep this organism, which we identify as "me," safe and out of harm's way. On the positive side, fear is your first line of defense against threats. Had our ancestors been fearless, in the sense of having no fear whatsoever, they would've heard rustling in the woods and thought, "Oh, that's just Fred playing in the bushes again." This type of fearlessness would've gotten them all killed! Only because of fear did their minds connect the rustling in the bushes to a possible threat—perhaps a large, hungry tiger—alerting them with urgency to take the proper steps to escape to safety. In this sense, fear is an important aspect of the human experience; but more often than not its presence creates a great deal of problems.

When a healthy relationship to fear has not been cultivated, it can lead to irrational behaviors and even aggression. Many of the cruel, terrifying acts of humans harming other humans have been fear based. As we have sadly seen all too often, this overwhelming emotion has the ability to create separation, racism, hatred, and sometimes may even lead to violence. Clearly, learning to befriend fear, as difficult as it may be, is both important and necessary.

Here's the paradox: learning how to recognize, manage, and *live with* your fears will lead you to a life of fearlessness. As you begin looking honestly at yourself, what you encounter may sometimes be quite frightening and will no doubt conjure up feelings of anxiety, nervousness, and other overwhelming emotions. Just because your brain is hardwired to fear doesn't mean you can't rise above your instincts and look beyond. In other words, you will always be fearful of something, but it doesn't have to hold you back or limit your responses during life's scariest moments.

Was President Franklin Roosevelt correct when he said, "The only thing we have to fear is fear itself"? Personally, I believe he hit the nail on the head. Fear is simply your emotional response to a situation. Are you afraid of death? Are you afraid of not being good enough? Are you fearful of never finding love or acceptance? We may not all have the same fears, but we all share the discomfort of fear when it manifests itself. Making friends with the "fear itself" is the path to fearlessness.

One great method I've learned for working with fear is called RAIN—an acronym for: Recognize, Accept, Investigate, and Nonidentify. Applying this practice can transform your difficulties and struggles, and it is a powerful on-the-spot practice that can help you become intimate with fear, in all its forms.

As with most methods, the prerequisite for this practice is simply to pay attention. Constant mindfulness of what's going on in your body and mind throughout the day will allow you to notice when certain causes and conditions begin stirring up fear. As discussed in the chapter about shenpa, catching difficult emotions such as fear in its early stages, as a little ember, makes it a lot easier to practice with.

The first step of RAIN is to *recognize* when something you hear, see, or think about has triggered an emotional contraction in your body. Once you recognize you have been set off into a fear-based conditioned response, you can *accept* that this has happened. Acceptance here means connecting with the direct experience of the present moment without the resistance from wishing it be some other way. Once you accept the presence of fear, the next step is to become curious and *investigate* it. Instead of just reacting to it, mindfully pause, and really observe the raw energy of it. Where are you experiencing it in your body? Where does it live? Your brain? Your heart? Your gut? Try to pinpoint the physical location of your fear, then breathe deeply, in and out, allowing the fear the space it needs to express itself. Remember, you're neither suppressing nor acting on the fear but, rather, curiously observing it so you can slowly begin to change the way you relate to it.

As you practice getting to know your fear when you experience it, you will naturally begin the last phase of RAIN: *nonidentifying*. By allowing the fear to be as it is, without trying to annihilate or grasp on to it, you are no longer identifying with it. The more you investigate it, the more you realize it's simply a conditioned response, and nothing more than an impermanent energy passing through the body. With this wisdom, you can allow it to arise and cease on its own, giving you the spaciousness to act freely and appropriately to the situation that set you off.

As you learn to become more in touch with fear, you'll find it does in fact have a healthy and appropriate place in your life. In certain situations it's actually pretty important and not something you want to simply throw away or try to annihilate. That being said, if you are able to understand the "fear itself" through the practice of RAIN, you may find better ways of relating to it. Remember, the path to actual happiness is not about getting rid of fear but, rather, learning to become most intimate with it.

22
A GOOD SENSE OF HUMOR

Teach us to care and not to care.
Teach us to sit still.

—T.S. ELIOT

IF THERE IS ONE THING you must have when
starting this journey, it's a good sense of humor.
Truly, a sense humor is the key to acceptance,
compassion, and wisdom. Humor will be your
best friend when things get tough, and it will
allow space in your mind for the problems of life
to float freely through, causing less harm to you
and those around you.

If you want to accept yourself, you need to be able to laugh at yourself. I cherish my friends so much because we can do this with the greatest of ease. Whenever I call my friend Jon for a pick-me-up, we launch into a little ditty that we composed for such an occasion. It plays off the Zen concept that your ordinary mind is itself a manifestation of the mind of Buddha—you just don't recognize it.

> If you're suffering, you're enlightened;
> If you feel like shit, that's nice,
> 'Cause if you feel like shit, and you don't
>   like it, guess what?
> You're enlightened! Tra-la-la-la-la. . . .

We know it's a silly song that has absolutely nothing whatsoever to do with the actual practice of Zen, but it sure does lift the burden facing us that day and creates a space for laughter where before there had been none.

Having a sense of humor is as simple as developing an open and playful attitude toward all aspects of your life. This is especially important with the practice of meditation. If you lack humor in your practice, you may tend to become too militant and hard on yourself. This is not the way of humor; instead, you can take your practice seriously enough to put in the effort of sitting and letting go of your thoughts, but if you miss a day, or if your mind is wandering all over, it's no big deal.

A sense of humor is like having what Shunryu Suzuki calls a beginner's mind—an eager and open mind without preconceptions or expectations. In his book *Zen Mind, Beginner's Mind* he states, "In the beginner's mind there are many possibilities, but in the expert's mind there are few." I see people in the yoga world who lack this beginner's mind or humorous approach to their practice. I call them the hardcore yogis. Hardcore yogis are people who believe they are very "advanced" practitioners. They come to class with their full-blown yoga mat and attire, along with their own high expectations of what the class *should* be. If it's not as they want it, they become miserable, get all worked up, and complain. They are unable to learn new things and appreciate a class done in a different way. I prefer to have students with beginner's minds at my yoga studio, and luckily, that's basically what I have because most of them started their yoga journey with me and are, in fact, beginners! It's wonderful because they don't expect my class to be a certain way, and we are able to joyfully practice together—this is the purpose of having a good sense of humor.

Having a sense of humor can be a blessing. It certainly makes difficult times more bearable and joyful ones even better. Sometimes a humorous event such as an unexpected surprise during an overly serious moment can act as a reminder to loosen up. For example, I was on a silent retreat that was becoming very intense. It was probably around the third or fourth day, and we were all sitting in a circle, vigorously focusing on our breathing. The room was very still, and all the participants were deep in concentration . . . except for one. Although I was fully present—as a good little meditator should be—I distinctly remember hearing someone slowly getting up and creeping out of the meditation hall. I didn't think much of it until a few moments later when a burst of explosive farts rang through the entire room from the bathroom; the only thing standing between us and the sounds of his gassiness was a thin veil over an open door.

Imagine hearing the echoes of flatulence reverberating in the toilet bowl! A number of people erupted into laughter, including me (of course), abandoning the discipline they were trying to achieve, while others tightened their lips in order to conceal their amusement. Although I couldn't see him, I am willing to bet that even the teacher cracked a slight smile (at least inwardly), as in that moment he too was reminded to relax, laugh, and appreciate the humor in the situation, however immature. In retrospect, I don't think any of us knew it was going to be more akin to a "silent but deadly" retreat! Clearly this one individual was literally pushing too hard to be his shitty, foolish self.

A good sense of humor is finding the right balance in both your meditation practice and your life in general. There's a story of a famous sitar player who was interested in studying meditation under the Buddha. Confused by his understanding of meditation, the musician asked the Buddha if he should try controlling his mind or just let it go completely. The Buddha replied by asking him how it was that he tuned the strings on his sitar. The musician explained that if he tuned the strings too tightly, they would just snap and break; yet if he strung them too loosely, the instrument wouldn't even make a sound. Only when the musician achieved the proper balance would the instrument be free to play its beautiful music. The Buddha wisely explained that it was the same with his meditation practice. And so it is with anything in your life. You must have a sincere effort and dedication to the practice, while simultaneously allowing enough space to not take it so seriously. Tune your strings so that you can sing your unique song, and don't forget to laugh along the way.

23
HONESTY &
GENTLENESS

*The most fundamental aggression to
ourselves, the most fundamental harm
we can do to ourselves, is to remain igno-
rant by not having the courage and the
respect to look at ourselves honestly and
gently.*

—PEMA CHÖDRÖN

A S YOU BEGIN WORKING with meditation practice, you will start to become aware of all the
various emotions, thoughts, and story lines that
make up who you are. This is an opportunity to

learn what keeps you awake and open and what shuts you down and traps you in ignorance and confusion. Over time, and with mindfulness, you will begin to see the glorious parts of yourself along with the undesirable ones. It is this awakening and awareness that become the foundation of honesty and gentleness.

Being very clear about who you are, not just who you want or portray yourself to be, is an important aspect of living a more peaceful life. Once you start to know yourself, you can make friends with yourself. You can become your own best friend, actually, enjoying your company through the good moments and the bad. As your self-awareness increases, you will find that there aren't as many surprises in your emotional world—the same internal old friends come by again and again—and any surprises that do arise can be observed and learned about in a beneficial way. When you honestly know yourself completely, you know what makes you tick and what causes you to explode. You also understand what brings out your loving and compassionate side. Being honest is about exposing yourself completely, making friends with what you find, and saying both proudly and humbly, "This is who I am."

There is one problem, though, that I have found with pure honesty alone, and that is the self-hatred and aversion that come along with it. This is what usually happens: You start practicing meditation and become mindful of your emotions, actions, thoughts, and so on. You quickly realize your imperfections and become extremely dissatisfied with what you see. You can't stand how you act toward your significant other. You hate your addictions, your reactivities. You don't want to feel depressed and anxious. You can't stop worrying about money. You hate how your mind will never slow down. Is any of this sounding familiar? Although there are plenty of other, beautiful, aspects that make up who you are, all you can seem to focus on are the "bad" ones.

In his book *Who Ordered This Truckload of Dung?* the Buddhist monk Ajahn Brahm recalls a story that illustrates how we tend to focus only on the "bad" parts of ourselves. In the story, Ajahn Brahm was building a brick wall for the monastery in which he was living. After much hard work aligning and realigning each brick, Ajahn Brahm finally completed building the wall. He soon realized that every single brick was lined up perfectly *except* for two that were inclined on an angle. These two bad bricks bothered him so much that he met with the abbot of the monastery and offered to redo the entire wall. Of course, the abbot kindly refused his offer. After that, every time Ajahn Brahm had to walk past the wall, all he could see were the two bad bricks. One day a man came to visit the monastery, saw the wall Ajahn Brahm had built, and told him how nice it looked. Ajahn Brahm, in disbelief, couldn't accept the visitor's compliment and quickly brought his attention to the two bad bricks, explaining how the wall wasn't nice at all. The visitor acknowledged the two bad bricks but wisely pointed out the other 998 bricks that were lined up perfectly. This one man's comment had a great impact on Ajahn Brahm's perspective on the wall and, ultimately, on his life.

How is this story relevant to you? Take a look at yourself. How often do you focus solely on your "two bad bricks"? Are those "bricks" the only parts of you that you recognize and dwell on? Of course they aren't, but focusing only on the negative seems to be a deeply engrained habit in most people. This is where the concept of gentleness comes into play.

Honesty without gentleness can be like a hard slap to the face and may take you on a destructive path where the focus becomes stuck on the undesirable qualities that you find. Gentleness is your ability to hold what you find with compassion, rid of self-judgment. It's a way to befriend the parts of yourself that you wish would just disappear, and it's a way to connect with the vulnerability of being human.

So what does this look like in practice? It's easy to say, "Be gentle," but what does that mean? Gentleness is a kind, compassionate, and forgiving approach necessary for exploring your inner self. It is an open, nonjudgmental attitude toward all parts of yourself—not just the negative. Let's say you're unhappy with how you look. A friend comes along and compliments you on an outfit that appears well put together, but your first instinct is to not accept the compliment. In this instance your focus is on your "bad brick," and you cannot see beyond it. You need to get over that and accept the rest of the "wall." Admire the whole of you, which includes your perfections *and* your imperfections. If others choose to see the goodness in you, why can't you practice gentleness and do the same?

24
TWO SIDES, ONE COIN

*Nobody's life is entirely free of pain and
sorrow. Isn't it a question of learning to
live with them rather than trying to avoid
them?*

—ECKHART TOLLE

THERE'S AN OLD ZEN STORY of an aged Chinese
farmer whose horse escaped through a break
in its fence. The neighbors of the farmer heard
the news and told him how this was bad luck, for
he wouldn't have a horse to help him during the
planting season. The farmer replied, "Well, who

knows? Who can say?" A couple of days later, the horse returned with two wild horses, and this time when the neighbors heard about this, they told him he had great fortune. Again, the farmer replied, "Who can say?" The next day, the farmer's son was trying to tame one of the wild horses and fell off, breaking his leg. The neighbors heard about this and again told the farmer how this was such bad luck. As always, the wise farmer responded with, "Who can say?" That same day the king's army rode into town and took the eldest son of every family to be sent to war. Only the farmer's son remained because of his broken leg. Good fortune? Bad fortune? Who can say?

This short story shows how most people normally see the world with black-and-white thinking. Things are either good or bad, right or wrong, and so on. Your thinking mind is constantly labeling and judging your experience in this way, yet the truth is we don't have a crystal ball to see how things will turn out. You must learn to embrace all things as they come, because you never know if your "worst" moments are really your best, and vice versa. It's kind of like breathing. Every breath you take has an inhale and an exhale—two completely opposite motions to make up one complete breath. If you were to embrace only the wonderful, pleasurable moments in your life, while looking down on and trying to dismiss and avoid the harder times, it would be like trying to constantly inhale. Go ahead: do it. It won't be long before you realize that you're turning blue and need to breathe out. Inhales and exhales, in and of themselves, are neither good nor bad, right nor wrong; they're simply two necessary components of a complete breath. In the same way, the "good" and "bad" aspects of your life are not really limited to your thinking mind's interpretations but are actually just essential parts of a complete life. Worst, best; right, wrong; good, bad; pain, pleasure—these are all two sides of one coin. One cannot exist without the other, and this goes for all pairs of opposites. Of course it's fine to have these distinctions as a way to function in the world and keep a good conversation going, but you must always keep in mind that with one comes the other, and the reality or truth is beyond our descriptions, judgments, and discriminations.

With mindfulness and meditation you may begin to see each moment of your life as it is, rather than how your thinking mind is interpreting it. With this clarity you may learn to accept and rest in the good and the bad equally, not growing overexcited when things are going the way you'd like and not becoming extremely lost and upset when they aren't. When you decide to live your life completely awake, equally accepting pain and pleasure, gain and loss, and so on, you may find yourself sometimes feeling quite uncomfortable. Unfortunately, discomfort is part of the journey, and the sooner you are able to get comfortable with it, the better. In fact, it is during these uncomfortable times that you are able to learn and grow the most.

Discomfort and comfort are two sides of this one life we live, so welcome them both with open arms. Don't be like the neighbor of the Chinese farmer, always caught in the roller coaster of good and bad fortune. There's no way to know where any given experience will lead you, so instead, keep your eyes open and find out for yourself! What will today bring? Who knows? Who can say?

25
CLARITY, NOT PERFECTION

A flower falls, even though we love it;
and a weed grows, even though we do not
love it.

—DOGEN ZENJI

THE MAIN POINT of being your shitty, foolish self is not to become a perfected version of yourself or live an idealized life but to be clear as to what is *really* happening. What is your life *really* like? What are your relationships *really* like? Who are you *really*, right now in this moment? When you are clear about what *is*, rather than what you wish to be, there will be clarity, peace, and wisdom.

Instead of trying to change yourself or a situation, first try becoming clear as to what's really happening, and realize that your life will not always go according to *your* plan, which is "perfectly" all right. As Bruce Hornsby once sang, "That's just the way it is. . . ." With clarity on your side you will be very aware of what's happening, and you will act appropriately to bring about the least amount of suffering for yourself and others.

Remember, actual happiness comes not from changing the outer circumstances but from accepting what's true, working with it, and learning to rest in your natural wisdom. Be clear and accepting of what's present, and let go of the desire for things to be some other way. Give your mind the space it needs to live a fulfilling life, and remember you are not trying to be perfect— just practicing how to be clear and honest about what's happening right now, and working with what you find, rather than fighting against it.

Pema Chödrön writes, "As long as our orientation is toward perfection or success, we will never learn about unconditional friendship with ourselves, nor will we find compassion." That's the message of this book too. Stop trying so hard, and instead wake up to your life, just the way it is. Use everything as a means to cultivate wisdom and compassion, and remember, even clearly seeing your stuckness and struggles can allow you to become more intimate with what it means to be human. Use these times to grow compassion for all beings as well, and inspire others to get unstuck, guiding them with what has worked best for you. Although you will never be flawless, and you will absolutely make mistakes from time to time, you have the freedom to love yourself anyway. As Suzuki Roshi said so beautifully, "Each of you is perfect the way you are . . . and you can use a little improvement." This peaceful, accepting approach, as radical as it may seem, is what being your shitty, foolish self is all about, and what will truly transform your life. I hope you take these teachings to heart and finally find the actual happiness you've been searching for.

Good luck, my friend.

AFTERWORD

I**T'S SUCH A RELIEF** when it dawns on you that you can just be your shitty, foolish self—that in a profoundly important way, you really are already good enough. If you are willing to live this truth, then you will no longer be burdened with the guilt and frustration of trying so hard to fix or perfect yourself. Through the practices of meditation and mindfulness you will start to see all aspects of yourself and create enough space in your mind to hold them all with compassion. Seeing yourself clearly, you can then say yes and fully accept what you find. From this place of acceptance and compassion you can begin working with your life in a practical way that will lessen suffering for yourself and others. With more awareness in your daily life you will also find that happiness based on material goods is only a temporary and fleeting condition, and although I encourage you to thoroughly enjoy things as they come to you,

you no longer have to strive to attain and maintain those warm-puppy feelings. You can learn to be content with what you have, still enjoy the material goods of the world (while understanding their limits), and, I hope, choose to cultivate a path to peace. The actual happiness you are looking for is here, right now, and not in some future "better" place.

Although being your shitty, foolish self may seem like a lot of "doing nothing," such as mindful acceptance and seated meditation, there is definitely a lot of work to be done—constant work! You are going to need continuous awareness of each moment of your life. It's not just theories and practices for you to talk about or enjoy reading; it's a whole new way of being in the world—a beginner's mind, so to speak, that is eager to live each and every day without expectations or closed-mindedness. Mindfulness, meditation, compassion, shenpa . . . they're all part of the way of life that you might now be thinking about living. Although it may seem simple, it sure as hell is not easy at times, but then again, nothing worthwhile ever is. Your life is your path to awakening. Look into your reactions, thoughts, and emotions. Begin to simplify, slow down, and see clearly through mindfulness and meditation. Always remember to look at where you are, not where you want to be. Only in this moment can you try figuring out and working with your life situation.

It's hard to change, and it's almost impossible to plan for the unexpected events that happen to you. You may feel powerless, but you're not. You have the power to change your reaction to these things. Remember, if you can choose a course of action that promotes peace, no matter what you feel or experience, you are free. I always love to tell people that if they have a choice, they are free, and I sincerely believe this to be true. Obviously there are some things that we cannot choose, such as where we were born, our family, and so on, but our freedom lies not in the cards we were dealt but in what we decide to do with them. Right now you have the freedom to choose how you respond. What will that choice be? Will you decide to begin practicing meditation or to not make time in your busy day? Will you pick compassion or aggression? Will you choose to breathe in the suffering of others so that you yourself may be free of your own self-concern, or will you simply ignore it? The time to make a choice is now.

Remember, life is full of both pain and pleasure. Just because you may have uncomfortable feelings sometimes doesn't mean you're not supposed to have them. They are supposed to be there. Every one of us experiences them. You are not alone! You need to find a way to accept them while learning about yourself in the process. As you learn more about yourself, you will learn more about others. We all experience the various human emotions. Find meaning in what is happening inside and outside you right now. Share the pleasant experiences and cultivate compassion with the painful ones.

Whatever you feel right now is fine and can be used as a path to awakening. You are allowed to feel bad sometimes. Things fall apart, and that never feels good! You are not doing something wrong or being punished. It's all part of the human experience. It's how we grow. Your life is not bad; it never has been and never will be. Your thoughts, concepts, and judgments just make it seem that way sometimes. You must awaken to this moment and not get caught up in story lines that limit how much you experience the beauty of life. You will find peace. As I was once told, "There is no way to peace—peace *is* the way."

Peace and acceptance are already here right now. They are the deepest part of who you are—your natural wisdom. Acknowledge and embrace your fears and become fearless, and more importantly, always remember: it *is* okay to be your shitty, foolish self.

May you be free from all your suffering
and the causes of suffering.

May you become a peaceful warrior who
willingly and openly faces yourself and your life
with unwavering courage and curiosity.

May you find out the truth of who you are
and be comfortable being fully and completely your
"shitty, foolish self."

I wish you well on your journey.

ACKNOWLEDGMENTS

I AM INDEBTED TO the many enlightened individuals, both past and present, who have blessed me with the gift of their wisdom, teachings, and inspiration. I am grateful to those who have contributed to the changes I have made in my own life, some of whom I've had the honor to meet and others who have spoken to me through the pages of their own insightful books. I would be remiss if I didn't acknowledge them here personally and thank them for their guidance and inspiration:

To Rich Bohan, my sports massage therapy instructor from Healing Hands Institute and close friend, for leading me to my spiritual path by first introducing me to the practice of meditation.

To Dharma Drum Retreat Center, which has allowed me the silence and solitude necessary to cultivate mindfulness, wisdom, and peace.

To Joan Hoeberichts and the Heart Circle Sangha, Simon Child, Chang Wen Fashi, Pema

Chödrön, Jack Kornfield, Thich Nhat Hanh, Ajahn Brahm, Dzigar Kongtrül, Eckhart Tolle, and many other teachers, for their inspiring words and for encouraging me to continue with my practice of wisdom and compassion.

To Master Sheng Yen, Chögyam Trungpa Rinpoche, Ajahn Chah, and all other deceased teachers who have passed their wisdom down throughout the generations.

To Regina Guth, my family friend and first editor, who had the patience to sit with me through the entire journey of writing this book. To David Gettis for his creativity, hard work, and dedication throughout the publishing process of the initial edition of this book. To my beautiful wife, Michelle, and my children, Mason and Madelyn, for supporting everything I do and putting up with my absence during the many hours of solitude and writing.

To all friends and family for all their love and support.

BIBLIOGRAPHY AND RECOMMENDATIONS

Boorstein, Sylvia. *Don't Just Do Something, Sit There: A Mindfulness Retreat with Sylvia Boorstein.* San Francisco: HarperSanFrancisco, 1996.

Brahm, Ajahn. *Who Ordered This Truckload of Dung?: Inspiring Stories for Welcoming Life's Difficulties.* Boston: Wisdom Publications, 2005.

Chah, Ajahn. *Food for the Heart: The Collected Teachings of Ajahn Chah.* Boston: Wisdom Publications, 2002.

Chödrön, Pema. *The Places That Scare You: A Guide to Fearlessness in Difficult Times.* Boston: Shambhala, 2001.

———. *When Things Fall Apart: Heart Advice for Difficult Times.* Boston: Shambhala, 1997.

Chödrön, Pema, and Joan Duncan Oliver. *Living Beautifully with Uncertainty and Change*. Boston: Shambhala, 2012.

Kongtrül, Dzigar. *Light Comes Through: Buddhist Teachings on Awakening to Our Natural Intelligence*. Boston: Shambhala, 2008.

Kornfield, Jack. *After the Ecstasy, the Laundry: How the Heart Grows Wise on the Spiritual Path*. New York: Bantam, 2000.

————. *Bringing Home the Dharma: Awakening Right Where You Are*. Boston: Shambhala, 2011.

Kornfield, Jack, and Paul Breiter. *A Still Forest Pool: The Insight Meditation of Achaan Chah*. Wheaton, IL: Theosophical Publishing House, 1985.

Mattis-Namgyel, Elizabeth. *The Power of an Open Question: The Buddha's Path to Freedom*. Boston: Shambhala, 2010.

Mingyur, Yongey, Eric Swanson, and Daniel Goleman. *The Joy of Living: Unlocking the Secret and Science of Happiness*. New York: Harmony, 2007.

Nepo, Mark. *The Book of Awakening: Having the Life You Want by Being Present to the Life You Have*. Berkeley, CA: Conari, 2000.

Suzuki, Shunryu, and Trudy Dixon. *Zen Mind, Beginner's Mind*. New York: Walker/ Weatherhill, 1970.

Tolle, Eckhart. *The Power of Now: A Guide to Spiritual Enlightenment*. Novato, CA: New World Library, 1999.

Trungpa, Chögyam, and Sherab Chödzin. *The Path Is the Goal: A Basic Handbook of Buddhist Meditation*. Boston: Shambhala, 1995.

Warner, Brad. *Hardcore Zen: Punk Rock, Monster Movies, & the Truth about Reality*. Boston: Wisdom Publications, 2003.

INDEX

ABOUT THE AUTHOR

Mark Van Buren is a mindful-living trainer, yoga/meditation instructor, personal trainer, and musician who has been promoting health and wellness for over a decade. He has run dozens of workshops and retreats all over the Tri-State Area, and has been asked to speak at numerous colleges, including Columbia, Montclair State, and Bergen Community. A handful of yoga studios have already opened their doors to his message, allowing him to give talks and run guided meditations and retreats.

He has worked extensively with children and adults with autism and other special needs and has even released two solo albums, based on his inward journey through meditation, under the band name "Seeking the Seeker." Van Buren holds a bachelor of arts in religious studies from Montclair State University and two associate degrees from Bergen Community College, in exercise science and music, respectively. He is currently the owner and head instructor of Live Free Yoga Studio in River Edge, New Jersey.

WHAT TO READ NEXT FROM WISDOM PUBLICATIONS

I Wanna Be Well
How a Punk Found Peace and You Can Too
Miguel Chen with Rod Meade Sperry

"Miguel demonstrates a tangible spiritual practice grounded in reality that is available anywhere, anytime—and Miguel lets us know that we too can be well."—Sharon Salzberg, author of *Real Love*

Hardcore Zen
Punk Rock, Monster Movies, and the Truth About Reality
Brad Warner

"*Hardcore Zen* is to Buddhism what the Ramones were to rock and roll: A clear-cut, no-bulls**t offering of truth."—Miguel Chen, Teenage Bottlerocket

Saltwater Buddha

A Surfer's Quest to Find Zen on the Sea
Jaimal Yogis

"Heartfelt, honest, and deceptively simple. It's great stuff with the words 'Cult Classic' stamped all over it."—Alex Wade, author of *Surf Nation*

About Wisdom Publications

Wisdom Publications is the leading publisher of classic and contemporary Buddhist books and practical works on mindfulness. To learn more about us or to explore our other books, please visit our website at wisdompubs.org or contact us at the address below.

Wisdom Publications
199 Elm Street
Somerville, MA 02144 USA

We are a 501(c)(3) organization, and donations in support of our mission are tax deductible.

Wisdom Publications is affiliated with the Foundation for the Preservation of the Mahayana Tradition (FPMT).